The Path to Inner Peace

Mastering Karma

The Path to Inner Peace

Mastering Karma

Subhash Jain

MANTRA BOOKS

Winchester, UK
Washington, USA

JOHN HUNT PUBLISHING

First published by Mantra Books, 2022
Mantra Books is an imprint of John Hunt Publishing Ltd., No. 3 East Street, Alresford
Hampshire SO24 9EE, UK
office@jhpbooks.com
www.johnhuntpublishing.com
www.mantra-books.net

For distributor details and how to order please visit the 'Ordering' section on our website.

Text copyright: Subhash Jain 2021

ISBN: 978 1 80341 020 3
978 1 80341 021 0 (ebook)
Library of Congress Control Number: 2021915273

A CIP catalogue record for this book is available from the British Library.

Design: Matthew Greenfield

UK: Printed and bound by CPI Group (UK) Ltd, Croydon, CR0 4YY
Printed in North America by CPI GPS partners

We operate a distinctive and ethical publishing philosophy in
all areas of our business, from our global network of authors to
production and worldwide distribution.

Contents

Preface

In our daily lives, we identify people by how they are physically different from one another. However, identical twins can be differentiated from each other by functional dissimilarities. In other words, human beings (as well as other types of living beings) are different from each other because they perform different actions. Our actions make every one of us unique. Our actions define us. We are the sum total of the consequences of our actions. Every action has consequences, which the performer of the action must bear. The proverb "As you sow, so you shall reap" captures this inviolable law of nature. No wonder almost all religions in the world preach some form of this belief. In Indian religions, this axiom is called the "karma doctrine."

The word "karma" has become a part of the daily vocabulary of the western world for the last few decades, as Westerners have started showing interest in it. But many people, including most Westerners, are skeptical of the karma doctrine because the various existing models are alleged to suffer from inconsistencies and controversies. This book, which presents the fundamentals of the karma doctrine, offers a model that is assumed to be free from inconsistencies with its unique explanation of the karma doctrine and its discussion of the natural laws of the karma-doctrine-governed consequences of actions and their effects on living beings.

Not all consequences of actions are governed by the karma doctrine. Two types of consequences of actions are identified — universal consequences and environmental consequences. Only universal consequences of actions are governed by the karma doctrine. In Chapter 6 we will discuss why the same is not true of environmental consequences. This distinction eliminates the inconsistencies that have plagued the doctrine in the past. Once we understand these natural laws, we can become the master of our destiny by managing our actions and following the path to inner peace.

The book presents the fundamental principles of the karma doctrine through a fictional account of the relationship between a guru and his American student. As the story unfolds, the guru instructs the student on how "karmic debt" is incurred as the result of personal action and how this "debt" can be reduced through behavioral choices. With an emphasis on nonviolent action, the guru elucidates the path whereby karmic attachment is decreased, leading to inner peace. The book presents an in-depth analysis of actions that lead to karmic attachment, how to avoid karmic attachment, and what the consequences of karmic attachment are. The issues of free will vs. determinism and good vs. evil are also dealt with in detail.

The metaphysical model of the karma doctrine includes a few technical terms that are defined at the point of their initial appearance in the text and are included in the Glossary for reference.

Acknowledgments

The author has drawn material for the book from his Ph. D. dissertation and wishes to thank Supervisor Dr. Priyadarshana Jain, Department of Jainology, University of Madras, Chennai, for her valuable guidance during the research work. The author is greatly obliged to a good friend, Ms. Patricia Ryan, for providing comments that made it significantly easier to clarify the concepts in the book for Westerner readers. The author is also very grateful to his family members, late wife, Kaushalya Jain, in particular, for their support.

Chapter 1

Ways to Understand Karma

I know camping alone for the summer at Yellowstone National Park wouldn't be everyone's way to celebrate graduation from high school. And believe me, as the only offspring, ("kid" doesn't sound right anymore), in the family, I had to do some talking to convince my parents that I knew how to protect myself—you know, from bears and the occasional unsavory member of the human species. The day I left our home in San Jose, California, I pretended not to see the tears in my mother's eyes.

It's been cloudy for the last few nights, but the sky is clear this Saturday night. I'm lying in my tent and watching the stars appear in the indigo sky through a screen in the center of my tent, thinking about the lecture my high school physics teacher gave about the Big Bang Theory. It claims the universe was created sometime between 10 billion and 20 billion years ago from a cosmic explosion that hurled matter in all directions.

A "shooting" star in the sky distracts me for a few minutes from thinking about the physics lecture, but then I find myself wondering why both parents and religions preach that one must do good things. This thought brings to mind a teaching I read in a book on karma last summer. The book was given to me by one of my best friends, Ajay Jain, who practices Jainism. He and I occasionally have had thought-provoking chats on karma. Before meeting Ajay four years ago in high school, I'd never heard of the Jain religion. Ajay informed me that Jainism is a fully-developed and well-established religion indigenous to India, where three other religions—Hinduism, Buddhism, and Sikhism—also originated. He said that modern historians credit Mahavira, a monk who was a contemporary of Gautama Buddha, with re-establishing the ancient religion Jainism in the

6th century BC. According to Ajay, though Jainism has some features in common with Buddhism and Hinduism, it has many distinctive insights, especially the salient features of the karma doctrine, that distinguish it from these other religions. Ajay and I once visited the Jain temple that was built recently in Milpitas, CA.

According to the book on karma, its theory is based on a metaphysical presupposition that good actions give rise to desirable consequences, and that evil actions result in undesirable consequences. The book's logic has convinced me that this metaphysical presupposition is the basis of a fundamental tenet which has universal acceptance. The tenet has been expressed in diverse ways in various sayings, such as "As you sow, so shall ye reap," "Every action has a reaction," "What goes around, comes around," "You bear the fruits of your karma," and so on. In Indian philosophy, this tenet is known as the karma doctrine, and it is one of the main tenets of Jainism. The karma doctrine is a law of cause and effect, which asserts that every action has consequences. An action is the cause, its consequences are the effect, and the doer of the action bears its consequences. According to Jainism, the karma doctrine is based on this law of nature that no living being can violate.

At this point in my life, I feel a need to find my own path that will bring spiritual transformation and expanded inner resources. As my Western culture's spiritual tradition repudiates reincarnation, and hence actions in past lives, my upbringing has not included any understanding of the universal karma doctrine as elementary to the soul's journey and human life. Still, I find the karma doctrine intriguing, and I feel it could be a missing piece of my path. That's why I want to delve into this enigmatic karmic process before entering college, where a normative Western lifestyle will surely prevail.

I understood rudimentary concepts of the theory of karma from the book. The book asserts that we perform actions twenty-four hours a day, seven days a week, and that as a matter of fact, that's the only thing we do all the time. The dissimilarity among our actions distinguishes one individual from another. Although the physical dissimilarities among our bodies also help make distinctions among us, this may not be true for identical twin children or for the few clone animals that researchers have produced. Even for identical twins, there are functional dissimilarities between them. The parents of identical twins can easily tell them apart based on the twins' actions. And even for two clones in a litter of cloned mice, actions are dissimilar. One might be running around the cage while another is just resting. In other words, every living being is distinct from others because its actions are different from others. The actions of a living being make that living being unique.

There must be a reason why everybody's actions are different from others. This reason cannot be genetic because the DNAs of identical twins and clone animals are identical. I wonder if the law of karma can explain this. More questions come to mind, too. Innumerable living beings, including millions of human beings, are born and die every year in the world. Where do these living beings come from? Where do they go after death? Will the soul of a human being after death come back in the new body of a human or some other being?

Ajay told me that Buddhists and Jains believe in reincarnation; and that, for the karma doctrine to be meaningful, the presupposition of rebirth is indispensable. This makes me wonder if the soul of a living being can liberate itself from the cycle of birth and death. If so, how? Does liberation from the cycle of birth and death have to do with spiritual awakening? Does the karma doctrine provide guidance that leads to spiritual transformation and expansion of inner resources?

In addition to my queries regarding the rebirth of living beings, there are questions related to the vast heterogeneity in shapes and sizes of the bodies of living beings and in their characteristics. Why are some people born healthy while others ill, some intelligent while others mentally challenged, some compassionate while others cruel, some humble while others arrogant, and so on? According to Ajay, most Easterners have shown persistent interest over the centuries in answers to these questions, finding that the karma doctrine helps provide answers.

Many people think that the suffering and heterogeneity in this world cannot be understood, and that God has a plan that cannot be apprehended. But this is not convincing reasoning to a lot of people, and I'm one of them. I believe there must be a logical explanation for the suffering and heterogeneity in the world. That explanation may be found in the law of karma.

Then there's the issue of consequences of actions. Ajay presented the following example during our chat about a month back. Two persons stole some diamonds, but only one of the thieves was caught by the police. The person not caught by the police escaped with the diamonds; he went on to enjoy the life of a rich individual. The person caught was incarcerated and is living the life of a poor prisoner. While both thieves stole the diamonds, the consequences of the same action were different for each of them.

Can the difference in the consequences of their actions be explained by their past actions? For example, did the person who escaped being caught perform good actions in the past, while the person who went to prison perform evil actions? This explanation makes some sense but raises more questions. Why did the person who performed good actions in the past go on to commit the evil action of theft? Is it possible that all consequences of present actions aren't governed by the karma doctrine? If so, what type of consequences of present actions *are* governed by the karma doctrine? Are the present actions of human beings controlled by their past actions only? Is it possible that we really have no control over our present actions and hence no free will?

Ajay couldn't answer all my questions. However, he gave me a piece of paper with the telephone number of a person who has studied the karma doctrine in depth and is familiar with its intricacies. Ajay informed me that this person lives in Cody, WY, near Yellowstone National Park. I am contemplating giving him a call.

These are the kinds of pressing ideas I want to think about this summer, underneath the stars, before I jump into the hectic pace of college life at Stanford University that will include making new friends; studying for my physics and calculus classes; deciding if engineering is really *my* choice of major, not just my parents'; playing in the jazz band; and who knows what else. All that is going to distract me from these big questions.

You know, like *what's the purpose of all this anyway?* I'm talking about life—this life. Our lives. I mean, *why do terrible things happen to good people? How do we find inner peace?* It seems to me that such questions can only be resolved if we understand *why we perform different actions* in the first place. I really do think the answers might lie in the karma doctrine.

Am I the only eighteen-year-old who lies awake at night, thinking about these things? Okay, maybe I'm an old man already. But this is me. I want to explore the important questions of life and how the karma doctrine may help answer them before I plunge into a "rut" prescribed by traditions. That's why I decide that tomorrow I will call the number Ajay gave me.

I have a good night's sleep under the stars. I usually love the smell of vegetables cooking over a campfire, but this morning I rush the cooking in my haste to make the phone call. I hardly taste my sweet potato.

As soon as I've swallowed the last bite, I muster the courage to take my cell phone from my pocket and dial. After several rings, the pleasant voice of an older man says, "Hello; I am Guru speaking. How may I help you?"

I pause for a few seconds. "My name is Jason, and I'm a friend of Ajay Jain."

"Oh yes! Ajay told me all about you, and I was expecting your call. So, you want to study the karma doctrine. Tell me one thing; why do you need to study such a doctrine?" asks the man. He sounds a bit older than my father but not like an old man. Maybe he's in his sixties.

I'm not prepared for his scrutiny, even though I've been contemplating this question for a while now. I swallow and say, "I believe that there should be a law of nature that governs our actions. I want to understand the nitty-gritty of such a law. I'm starting college this fall and worry that I'll have no time to think philosophically about such things after that."

"I see," says Guru. "Where do you plan to attend college?"

"I plan to attend Stanford University in the fall," I reply.

Guru pauses and then says, "Every philosophical or religious tradition of India has developed the notion of karma into a model of the karma doctrine. However, none of the models is coherent and completely beyond reproach. The redevelopment of a model of the karma doctrine requires both reason and faith, as it is a metaphysical model. One can use different approaches to discover the metaphysical model, but one cannot necessarily acquire faith with each approach. Only after contemplation and reflection does one arrive at unconditional faith."

"There are basically three ways to understand the model," he continues. "You can follow the path I pursued. I spent ten years studying, contemplating, and reflecting on the model. As a result, I intuited the model myself, and I have a genuine faith in it. Though I had no teacher, I was fortunate to meet several intellectuals who helped me to clarify my reasoning and doubts. It could take you several years to discover the model yourself if you follow this path."

"What's the second path?" I ask.

"The second path is to read someone else's writings. For

example, you can read the booklet in which I have summarized my conclusions. It might take you only a few days to go through it, but it may not fully satisfy you and lead to faith, because some of the conclusions may not make sense to you without further dialogue and reflection. However, this is certainly a legitimate way to proceed, especially if you desire just a basic introduction at this point, with the idea that you will pursue deeper study in the future."

"What about the third path?"

"Jason, the third path is to intuit the model yourself but with the help of an experienced guide, such as myself. The knowledge and reason for understanding the model and acquiring faith in it can be transmitted within a month if you spend a couple of hours every day with me. I recommend the third path over the second path, because your wisdom and potential enlightenment will proceed more quickly. However, you can certainly read the booklet in case you decide to follow the second path. Think over these options and call me back when you are ready."

"Where will we meet if I decide to follow the third path?" I ask.

"You will come to my dwelling, which is a couple of miles outside of Cody on the highway that leads to Yellowstone National Park," replies Guru.

"When would we meet?" I ask.

"You can pick the time. I have flexible hours."

"Let me think about it; I'll call you back," I reply.

I put my cell phone back into my pocket as my mind grapples with the three paths described by Guru. The first path is not for me, as I can't afford to spend so much time pursuing the answer. I mean, my mother and father are generous, but they don't want to support me forever! The second path may be useful in gaining knowledge, but I have the sense that it will not answer all my questions or instill faith in me. I decide to pursue the third path. If I stay at the park, I can enjoy the park in the mornings and meet Guru for our daily discussion after lunch. I call him five minutes later.

He answers, "Yes, Jason." Somehow it surprises me that a man possessed of such ancient wisdom has caller ID and recognizes my phone number already! I tell him my plan. We agree to meet Monday through Friday between 1:00 pm and 3:00 pm, starting tomorrow. It'll mean some driving—about thirty minutes each way—but a sense of peace comes over me. I'm hungry again. I begin to fix myself some tea and a snack.

It looks like I'll be thinking about some deep stuff this summer. I begin to daydream about how, if Guru helps me understand the model of the karma doctrine, maybe I'll end up writing about it in a way that others can understand. If so, maybe someone will name a landform after me out here in Yellowstone, though it's probably the case that most landforms have names by now. Maybe a building on the Stanford Campus: The Jason Building. Yeah, I like the sound of that.

Chapter 2

General Nature of Substance

As I wake up a little late this morning, I rush through my usual breakfast and morning hike. It doesn't escape me, this irony of rushing through nature when I intended to immerse myself in it all summer while idly pondering the "big" questions.

It doesn't take me as long as I expected to reach the town of Cody. In fact, I arrive at Guru's dwelling a few minutes early. I carry a laptop in case I need to take notes.

Guru's home is a simple one-room wood-frame dwelling. The door is open, and I can see a man inside the room sitting in front of a low desk on a mat on the floor. I knock at the door. Guru smiles pleasantly and asks me to come inside. I leave my shoes outside and enter the room. A quick glance reveals just a few household items in the room, including a couple of books and a Webster's dictionary on the desk. Guru is wearing a loose, one-piece robe, and he has a long salt-and-pepper beard. He appears middle aged — about 60 — just as I had gauged from the sound of his voice on the phone. I notice an esoteric glow on his face, a kind of radiance one expects from a spiritually awakened person. I immediately sense that Ajay directed me to the proper guide.

"I'm Jason," I say. "I talked to you yesterday."

Guru nods his head and asks me to sit on the mat on the other side of the desk. "I see that you carry a laptop. Do you have access to the Internet?" he asks.

"Yes, at the local library. I'm camping at Yellowstone this summer."

"By yourself?"

I nod, and he nods back.

"You can find plenty of information on topics that will be

valuable to our discourse on the Internet. Will you have time to do research and still enjoy your stay at Yellowstone?"

"I believe so."

"I am pleased to hear that, Jason. Should we begin?"

I nod.

"In our discourse we will use logic based on common sense, and sometimes we will need to define terms that will be helpful in our discussion."

I nod.

He continues, "We will follow a logical procedure that involves three phases. The first phase entails learning a set of presuppositions that will serve as the foundation of the karma doctrine model. These presuppositions, like the presupposition of the existence of God in some other paradigms, can neither be proved nor disproved but must be considered true, or else the model would be meaningless. Based on these presuppositions, in the second phase we will discover a metaphysical model of the karma doctrine. Then in the third phase we will test the metaphysical model by applying it to examples from everyday life, including finding the path to inner peace that leads to liberation from the cycle of birth and death. We will explore many concepts having to do with spiritual awakening, reincarnation, free will, and several other topics. Do you understand?" asks Guru.

"I'm with you," I reply.

He stares at me intently. "I must warn you that the first two phases will be painstaking and, at times, laborious. However, as we apply our new learning to many aspects of our life process, it will all come together. Are you prepared for this arduous work?"

I take a deep breath as I acknowledge internally that I probably wasn't prepared to work so hard this summer before beginning my difficult classes at college this fall. But why not? Working hard intellectually this summer may just be exactly what I need to do. "I think I'm prepared," I reply.

He nods, smiles, and continues talking. "We live through many events so often that we do not consider it necessary to look for explanations of their occurrence. For example, every day we experience the phenomenon that anything which slips from our hands always goes down, never up. But it does not occur to us to look for an explanation for why things always go down, even though most of us do not understand gravitational law. Here is another example: We know of the birth of many children, but we never ask why they are here or where they came from. The occurrence of such events seems so natural that we take it for granted and never give it any deeper thought. Nonetheless, there are moments in every thinking person's life when it becomes necessary to find an explanation. You are going through such a moment in your life. Is that so?"

"I think so."

"Jason, I am pleased that you are here to study the karma doctrine. Most Westerners are skeptical about this doctrine because they have an inadequate understanding of it. Their ideas of the karmic process are erroneous, based on flawed concepts rather than on logical, realistic explanations. They have no idea which consequences of their actions are governed by the karma doctrine, and which are not."

Guru's remarks remind me of the time I asked Ajay whether all consequences of actions were governed by the karma doctrine. It seems Guru is going to address this question during our discourse.

Guru continues. "There are significant differences among the karma doctrines of different religions, as they are based on different presuppositions. A presupposition is something assumed to be true, without which any doctrine would be meaningless. Because the karma doctrine deals with living beings, the presuppositions of the karma doctrine are brought to light in the answers to the following two questions: 'What are the substances which living beings are made up of?' and 'Is there a cause for these substances?' In other words, 'Are these substances uncreated and eternal or is there a need for a creator to create them?' Before we seek the answers to these questions, it is very important that we first define the term 'substance,' as it has a specific meaning in relation to the karma doctrine."

I like this notion, this deliberate way of thinking. I already think I can learn from this teacher. I fire up my laptop so I can take notes. Guru pauses for a brief period while the machine whirs into action. He then begins to clarify the definition of the term "substance."

"I am going to take you on what may seem like a long tangent right now about 'substance.' You might make sure you are comfortable," says Guru.

I unfold my legs. I glance at Guru's folded legs on the other side of the desk. His robe covers his legs, but I can see their outline, and it looks like he's in that typical yoga position, with both legs folded and his feet folded into the crook of the opposite leg. I try to imitate him, and then I worry about how long I'm going to be able to keep the pose without killing my back.

Guru seems not to notice my discomfort and continues, "Substance is defined as that (i) which exists, (ii) which has properties and modes, and (iii) which is characterized by simultaneous origination of new modes, cessation of old modes, and permanence of intrinsic properties."

I didn't expect to be sitting here, talking about the word "substance" in such depth. What does that have to do with the karma doctrine? Is this a physics lesson, or philosophy, or psychology, or what? I feel lost, and now I'm not sure I should have committed to coming here five afternoons a week. I unfold my legs to let the pressure off my back, but Guru doesn't notice that I'm not keeping up with his posture.

"Can you name one substance?" he asks.

"My understanding is that any object or entity, such as the

book or the desk in this room, is a substance." I'm stabbing in the dark here, but I am energized by this conversation.

"Are the book and the desk in this room one substance or different?"

"The book is made of paper and the desk is made of wood, so they are two different substances."

"But the paper and the wood, in fact all physical objects, are composed of the same subatomic particles," explains Guru. "Hence all objects or things are different states of the properties, called mode, of the same substance. The mode is the state of properties of a substance that undergoes change. Do you know the name of that substance?"

"You must be referring to matter."

"Right! All physical objects are made of matter. According to my understanding and belief, the universe is composed of more than one substance; matter is only one of them. As we have some familiarity with matter, we will examine how the definition of substance I just described is applicable to matter. Now tell me, can matter be created or destroyed?"

The question takes my mind back to my high school physics class in which I learned that matter can neither be created nor destroyed.

"The answer for both is no. Matter can neither be created nor destroyed," I reply.

"That is correct. Logically, something which exists cannot become non-existent, and that which is non-existent cannot exist. This means that matter is indestructible and non-creatable. Following from this, we apply the presupposition that all other substances that constitute the universe are eternal and uncreated, also. There is, therefore, no need for a creator of substances and hence of the universe. This presupposition, which assumes that matter has always existed, is different from many religions. However, Buddhism and Jainism do not involve a creator/God. Do you have any questions about any of this?"

"Yes, if matter is eternal, why do we use the phrase, 'Nothing lasts forever?'" I ask.

"Very intelligent question: The word 'nothing' in the phrase refers to either a circumstance or an object. A well-wisher uses this phrase to console his or her friend who is going through a tough period. In such cases the word 'nothing' denotes a circumstance or an event that changes with time. But a circumstance or an event does not exist; it happens or occurs. In other words, the circumstance or the event is not a substance. The phrase is also used when an object breaks down. A friend might say, 'Don't worry, nothing lasts forever' when a ceramic pot shatters into pieces after falling on the hard floor. In this case the phrase implies that nothing lasts forever in the same mode. All things change with time. The ceramic pot may be shattered into shards of clay, which then break down into bits of clay which, over time, evolve into clay. Am I making myself clear?"

"Yes." I'm saying yes, but I'm not sure I really mean it.

Guru continues, "As there are multiple substances in the universe, what makes one substance distinct from others?"

I glance at the screen of my laptop to check the definition of a substance and note that a substance has properties.

"As a substance has properties, each substance must have some properties that other substances do not have; such properties must distinguish one substance from others," I reply.

"Very good, Jason. You perceive with your senses certain properties of matter in an object, and these properties help you to infer that the object is made of matter. What properties do you perceive with your senses?"

"Since I have five senses, I would say the properties I perceive with my senses are touch, taste, odor, color, and sound."

"Almost correct but not quite, Jason. Sound is not a property of matter; it is a form of energy. From the theory of relativity in physics we know that mass can be converted into energy. Matter exists not only in the form of solids, liquids, and gases, but also in the form of energies. Sound is considered a form of matter, not a property of matter. Matter has only four properties which are perceived by our senses: touch, taste, odor, and color. Matter cannot exist without these intrinsic properties. However, the unaided human senses cannot always perceive these intrinsic properties in all types of matter."

"Okay, that makes sense," I remark.

"Though these intrinsic properties are always present in matter, the modes of these properties change constantly with time. Some change at an imperceptible rate and others at a noticeable rate. Do you expect any changes in this book if it is left on this desk for a very long period—say, fifty years?" asks Guru.

"I've seen several old books in my school library. Their pages have turned brittle and yellowish in color. I expect the same would happen to this book."

"Is the change in the book occurring all the time?"

"I believe so."

"So, matter is therefore always undergoing modifications. Each entity in this room is undergoing changes. Change refers to the cessation of the old mode and the origination of the new mode at every instant. But what happens to the matter that makes up all of these entities?"

"I believe matter always remains matter."

"Very good, Jason. Matter does not lose its own intrinsic properties or assume the intrinsic properties of another substance. In other words, any one substance cannot be transformed into any other substance. The number of substances in the universe is fixed. The substances that constitute the universe undergo numerous processes through their interactions and modifications."

Guru continues, "Let us go back to the question related to the substances that constitute living beings. Since our body is made of matter, it has the intrinsic properties of touch, taste, odor, and color. But our body matter has additional properties, such as respiration, sensory capabilities, etc. Why does matter that comprises our bodies have more properties than matter that comprises the items in this room, such as the desk, mat, books, etc.?"

The question reminds me of the lesson in biology class, where I learned about two types of matter—living and nonliving.

"Our bodies are made of living matter, while the items in the room are made of nonliving matter," I reply.

Guru prompts, "Tell me the difference between the two."

"Living matter has consciousness and the ability to metabolize, grow, and reproduce. Nonliving matter does not have any of these capabilities."

"Jason, your answer raises several questions. Are we able to introduce these additional properties of living matter in nonliving matter? If not, do we need a substance other than matter to explain how these additional properties of living matter emerge? If so, what is the nature of this other substance? Tomorrow we will explore the answers to these questions."

I'm glad to learn that today's discourse is over because I feel like my brain's going to explode with the term "substance." At the very least, my legs are going to be stuck in place. I've absorbed about as much as I can today.

But Guru continues. "I am very pleased by your performance. If you find time, you can research the topics of DNA, philosophy of mind, and afterlife on the Internet."

"I'll try to do that and will see you tomorrow at the same time," I respond.

Guru offers me a cup of orange juice and some fruits. We both eat the food in complete silence. I glance at my watch; it's about 3 p.m. I take Guru's permission to leave, and he raises his hand in a gesture of blessing. I leave the room and put on my shoes.

It's very pleasant outside. I drive to the library to do my Internet research. I already had some knowledge of DNA from my biology class in high school. It takes me an hour to complete my assignment, and then I drive back to the camp site. My mind churns through our dialogue. Now that I have had time to reflect, I realize I understand most of what we talked about today. I hope Guru will review these complex concepts tomorrow.

Chapter 3

Constituents of Living Beings

My first interaction with Guru was motivating. I'm curious to discover the various substances that constitute the universe. I stare at the stars in the night. It seems that they're winking at me, saying "Jason, you're onto something here!" I dream that Guru's on a surfboard in the Pacific off the coast of San Diego, teaching me patiently to surf. In the morning I wake up smiling.

I reach the Guru's dwelling at the appointed time in the afternoon. He sits where he sat yesterday. I enter the room, after taking off my shoes, and take the same seat again.

Guru closes his eyes briefly and takes a long breath. "Every day before the discourse, we will summarize what we learned the previous day. Is it okay with you?" he asks.

"It's fine with me."

"Substance is that which exists and has properties and modes. It is eternal and uncreated; it just is, with no initial creator because it is eternal. Substance constantly undergoes modification, but during modification it maintains its intrinsic properties; hence one substance cannot turn into another substance. Any doubts?"

"Not at all!"

Guru breathes deeply again. "We need to identify the substances that compose living beings and the universe. You at least know one substance—matter. Do you know any other substances that exist in the universe?"

"I've been thinking about it since yesterday, but I can't imagine any substance other than matter."

"Your answer does not surprise me," says Guru, "because the recognition of the other substances is not as easy as that of matter. It is straightforward to identify matter in the universe, since it can be perceived through senses and available scientific tools. The additional substances that constitute the universe are non-physical and cannot be recognized by senses. The existence of non-physical substances in the universe can be inferred only by logical reasoning and by means of their functions. This mental process is likely to initiate some skepticism, but I am afraid we have no other choice. We can minimize or even circumvent skepticism by making use of careful logical reasoning."

"I hope so," I remark.

"Are you made of living matter only or is there another substance also that you are composed of?" asks Guru.

"I think I'm made of living matter only."

"Do you know the name of the basic biological unit of living matter?"

"You must be referring to the cell."

"Right! What are the main constituents of the cell?"

"The cell contains many biomolecules, such as proteins, nucleic acids (DNA, RNA), carbohydrates, and lipids." I feel proud of myself for knowing these things. I never knew when I called Guru two days ago that I'd be reviewing information from my high school biology classes. My parents would certainly be happy right now!

"Can scientists artificially create these constituents of the cell?"

"I believe so."

"Can these constituents be considered living matter?" asks Guru.

"No, these constituents are nonliving, since they can't grow or reproduce by themselves," I respond.

"How do these nonliving constituents get transformed into living matter?"

"The nonliving constituents get transformed into living matter only in *vivo*, i.e., in the living cell, not in *vitro*, i.e., not in the test tube."

"Excellent. Scientists have not yet artificially created a 'protocell.' They can transform nonliving constituents of the cell into living constituents in living cells only, not in test tubes."

"We will now consider another aspect of living matter. We have the capabilities of knowing, feeling, and willing; in other words, we have consciousness. Can consciousness be explained in physical terms?"

"Scientists consider consciousness to be one of the properties of the mind."

"Tell me whether you have a mind or not."

"Enough of a mind to be discussing highly abstract principles with you today, Guru, even though I have no idea where you're headed with this!" We both smile, and I continue, "Yes, of course; I do have a mind."

"What did you learn about the faculties of mind on the Internet?"

I pull up my notes on "mind" on my laptop and read aloud. "According to psychologists, mind has three main faculties: cognition, affection, and conation. Cognition is the mental action of acquiring knowledge; affection is the mental action of developing emotions such as love, desire, and fear; and conation is the mental action of making decisions that direct physical actions." I take a moment to register what I've read, and then I say, "And these faculties compose the mind's key property of consciousness. The three faculties of mind can be demonstrated with an illustration. Should I go ahead with the illustration?"

"Of course!"

"A man is strolling in the woods, and a wild dog runs towards him. Feeling threatened, he climbs a nearby tree. All three faculties of the mind are present in his reaction to the wild dog. His knowledge about the dog is the aspect of cognition; his feeling of fear and desire to avoid injury by the dog are aspects of affection; and his decision to climb the tree, as well as his physical action of climbing the tree, are aspects of conation.

Mind, of course, isn't an entity that can be divided into parts like this. I did that only to illustrate its characteristics."

"Very true; I now see why you have been admitted to Stanford University!"

We both smile, and I say, "Thanks."

"Is cognition a necessary condition for performing action?" asks Guru.

"I think so. The man might not have performed the action of climbing the tree unless he had knowledge about the dog."

"Can the action be performed in the absence of affection?"

"I don't think so. The man might not have climbed the tree without first experiencing fear and desire to avoid injury by the dog. All three faculties of the mind are essential for performing an action."

"Is mind made of living matter, or a nonphysical substance?" asks Guru.

"My research pointed out that scientists are divided into two groups on this issue. One group considers mind to be a part of the body and hence it's made of living matter. The other group believes that there are two types of mind: physical mind and non-physical mind. Physical mind is characterized by what it *does,* while non-physical mind is characterized by the way it *feels* as conscious experience. Consciousness is a property of a non-physical substance."

"Let's explore this non-physical substance a little more. Jason, what did you learn about afterlife on the Internet?"

"I found three main phenomena that support the existence of some type of afterlife: remembrance of past life, out-of-body and near-death experiences, and messages from the dead received through a medium. A very comprehensive study on remembrance of past life by children was conducted by the American psychologist Ian Stevenson, who methodically documented the children's statements about past life. He then identified the deceased person with whom the child claimed to identify and verified the facts of the deceased person's life that matched the child's memory. He concluded that the phenomenon of rebirth is the best explanation for these children's memories."

"From our discussion we can conclude that there are several questions which science is unable to resolve," Guru says. "Why does DNA work only in living cells, not in test tubes? The sensory nerves carry messages to the brain and record changes in it, but *who* receives these messages and perceives these changes? No doubt the brain is the main instrument for perception, command, and recollection, yet *who* operates through this mechanism? More than one thousand cases of persons who have given accounts of their previous lives have been reported, but *who* remembers the events of the past life? How does one explain parapsychic experiences like precognition, premonition, and extra sensory perception (ESP)?"

Guru continues, "Until scientists can supply answers to these questions and introduce consciousness in matter, we will have to work on the premises that consciousness is not a property of matter and living beings are not made of matter only. There is another substance, which has properties that are different from matter, that is also a constituent of living beings. Like many scientists and philosophers, we call this metaphysical substance 'soul.' Matter that has association with a soul, such as your bodily matter, is living matter; otherwise, it is nonliving matter. In other words, nonliving matter gets transformed into living matter after coming into association with the soul. Does this make sense to you?"

"Yes," I reply.

Guru continues, "My personal belief is in accord with those scientists who support two types of mind: physical mind and non-physical mind. The non-physical mind is soul, with consciousness as one of its properties. The physical mind is made of matter. Using the explanation of substances and living beings that we have been reviewing, karma doctrine is founded on the following presuppositions:

1. Living beings are made up of two substances, namely, matter and soul.
2. Substances are uncreated and eternal.
3. Since there is no beginning and no end, there is no creator.
4. Substances are differentiated from one another by their intrinsic properties.
5. Substances retain their intrinsic properties during modifications.
6. One substance does not change into another substance.
7. Nonliving matter transforms into living matter after coming into association with soul.

"Are you there with me?"

"I believe so." I say this slowly because the image of a frog pops up, or of an insect, and I find it remarkable that these creatures have souls.

As if to read my mind, Guru says, "I know there are in this world a few materialists who believe that the universe is composed of only matter and there is no such substance as soul. I hope you are not one of them. Are you?"

"No, I'm not."

"I am glad to hear that because the karma doctrine we are studying, and hence our discourse, has no relevance to materialists."

I always thought that there's only one substance—matter—in the universe. Now I know that there are at least two of them—matter and soul. "How many more substances are there in the universe?" I ask.

"Are you losing patience?"

"No, I am just curious to know."

"According to my understanding, Jason, the number of

substances that constitute the universe is six. Therefore, there are four more substances, in addition to soul and matter. Two of them are space and time. Space accommodates infinite physical objects and living beings, and time enables the experience of consecutive events. The four-dimensional continuum of space and time forms a finite universe beyond which no particle of matter or energy and no soul can travel but beyond this finite universe there is an infinite extension of space. However, the two additional substances are not crucial to discovering the model of karma doctrine. If time permits, we will discuss them after completing our study of the karma doctrine. Do you have any other questions related to matter or soul?"

"No." I'm relieved as I was getting tired of talking about substances.

"Tomorrow we will discuss the properties of soul and matter. Knowledge of their properties is essential to discovering the metaphysical model of the karma doctrine. For tomorrow's discourse I want you to research the topics 'matter' and 'soul' on the Internet. Do you think you can study these topics?"

"I believe so."

"We still have some time left, Jason. Would you like to visit my garden?"

"That would be wonderful."

We both roam in the garden for the remaining time. Guru's garden has two separate plots of land: one for flowers and the other for vegetables. His flower garden has a variety of hybrid roses, and his vegetable garden includes tomatoes, bell peppers, a variety of lettuces, and many other vegetables.

I leave for the library around 3 p.m., eager to study about matter and soul on the Internet. Once again, I skim and download the information. When I reach the campsite, I lie down, try to recall what I learned from Guru today, and begin preparing short notes for tomorrow's discussion.

Chapter 4

Properties of Matter and Soul

Today is Wednesday, and I'll have my third visit to Guru in the afternoon. I must admit that I don't feel any closer to discovering the karma doctrine today than I was before meeting Guru. My head has been swimming with discussions of substance, matter, and soul. Last night I dreamed that Guru's head was detached from his body but still kept talking! I know that even today, instead of finally getting to the karma doctrine, we will discuss the properties of soul and matter. Nevertheless, I believe that my first two visits to Guru were rewarding, and so I'm eagerly awaiting today's visit.

I arrive at the Guru's dwelling with my research on soul and matter stored in my laptop. The moment I sit on the mat, Guru asks me to summarize what we have learned so far. I've already made a summary because I had a hunch that Guru would ask me to do that. I turn on my laptop, open the file, and read.

"Living beings are made up of two independent substances — matter and soul. Both matter and soul maintain their intrinsic properties during modification and do not get transformed into another substance. Matter always remains matter, and soul always remains soul."

"Good. Today we will discuss some key properties of matter and soul," says Guru.

I interrupt Guru and ask, "What do the properties of matter and soul have to do with the karma doctrine?"

"Good question. According to the karma doctrine, the doer of an action bears the consequences of that action. How do you think the consequences of their actions affect the doer, who is made up of matter and soul?"

"Since the doer is made up of soul and matter, the

consequences of their actions must affect their soul and bodily matter?"

"You did not answer my question, Jason; you simply swapped the doer with their soul and matter. How do the consequences of their actions affect their soul and body, which have properties and modes?"

"Oh, so the soul and matter of their body must be affected by changing the modes of their properties. I guess I need to understand better what those properties are."

"There is the answer to your question. For example, your current action of studying the karma doctrine is affecting the mode of the property of knowledge of your soul. Similarly, the consequences of your actions affect the modes of the other properties of your soul and bodily matter. We, therefore, need to study the properties of matter and soul. Can you recall the intrinsic properties of matter, that is, those properties that are always part of the nature of matter?"

"Matter has four intrinsic properties of touch, taste, odor, and color."

"Jason, you remember them correctly. These intrinsic properties of touch, taste, odor, and color, which are recognized by our sense organs, are some of the physical and chemical properties of matter, nonliving as well as living, identified by scientists. Living beings also have biological and psychological properties. Biological properties are the properties of living matter. Remember, nonliving matter becomes living matter after it comes into association with the soul. And psychological properties are properties of soul, not of living matter. For our discussion, we will divide matter, soul, and their properties each into two categories: living and nonliving matter, pure and worldly soul, and intrinsic and extrinsic properties. I have already defined living matter. Can you identify living and nonliving matter in the universe?"

"Since matter associated with soul is termed living matter,

bodies of living beings are made of living matter. The matter in the universe that has no association with soul is nonliving matter, e.g., all objects in this room."

"Can you define pure and worldly souls? To help you figure it out, you can think about the criterion for defining living and nonliving matter."

"Oh, I get it. A soul that has association with living matter is a worldly soul; otherwise it must be a pure soul."

"Good, Jason. A worldly soul has been in a state of transmigration, through reincarnation, from one lifeform to another in the past and will continue to do so until it liberates itself from association with matter and transforms into a pure soul. The purpose of human life is to achieve liberation from transmigration by transforming the imperfect worldly soul into a perfect pure soul."

"Wait a minute, Guru. This seems to be a very profound statement. Why would achieving liberation be our purpose?"

"Okay, Jason. You tell me the purpose of your life."

"According to me, the purpose of my life is to achieve happiness."

"What kind of happiness, temporary or everlasting?"

"Of course, everlasting."

"Where in the universe can you find it?"

"In heaven, if there is a heaven."

"Let us presuppose that there is a heaven. How do you transmigrate there?"

"If I perform good actions in my life, I will migrate to heaven after my death."

"Very well, Jason. We both are trying to achieve everlasting happiness. In the karmic model you are trying to intuit, a pure soul experiences everlasting happiness, while worldly souls, like ours, experience transient happiness. A worldly soul keeps transmigrating from one lifeform to another until liberation from transmigration when it becomes a pure soul."

"I understand now what you are trying to say. In the Judeo-

Christian tradition, there is only one life, but in the karmic model you keep cycling through births and deaths until your worldly soul becomes a pure soul."

"Yes. Okay, where was I? I defined two types of matter, living and nonliving, and two types of soul, worldly and pure. I need to talk about properties. Let me define intrinsic properties. The properties that are always present in a substance are intrinsic properties. In other words, a substance cannot exist without its intrinsic properties. We already know that matter, living as well as nonliving, has four intrinsic properties of touch, taste, odor, and color. These intrinsic properties are always present in matter; it cannot exist without them. Using the definition of intrinsic properties, can you define extrinsic properties?"

"I guess that additional properties that are only sometimes present in a substance are extrinsic properties. In other words, a substance can exist without the extrinsic properties."

"Excellent, Jason. Since living matter has properties besides those intrinsic properties shared with nonliving matter, these are extrinsic. The living matter of the physical body of a living being has extrinsic properties, but it loses them at the time of death and is transformed into nonliving matter. Similarly, a worldly soul has an extra extrinsic property, while associated with living matter, which it sheds when it transforms into a pure soul. The biological properties of living matter are extrinsic properties, as they do not manifest in nonliving matter. And we will learn one psychological property of worldly soul that is an extrinsic property, as it does not manifest in pure soul.

"As all living beings have the power of physical action, which is one type of biological property, let us first try to understand its nature. How do you perform physical actions?"

"I perform physical actions with my body. For example, I'm currently performing the physical action of sitting on a mat."

"You are also performing two additional types of physical actions—talking with your vocal organs and thinking with your mind. All three types of physical actions of body, vocal organs, and mind are present in the most highly advanced beings; less advanced beings have no mind and the least advanced have neither mind nor vocal organs. Therefore, they cannot do as many types of physical action."

Guru continues, "Bear with me. There are some things I need to explain that are going to take a little time, but it will make sense eventually. Is it okay with you if our discussion continues for a little longer period than usual?"

"That's fine with me."

"Biological properties are related to the physiology of living beings. Your current activity here in my dwelling is affecting the modes of the physiological properties of your body. For example, the environment, which includes everything in the room, is affecting the physical sensations of your sensory organs; the physical actions of your body, vocal organs, and mind; the lifespan of your body; and your health and operation of organs. Can you think of some ways in which your daily activities affect your body?"

"Let me think. Well, eating food each day affects my physical health, such as the strength of my immune system."

"Yes. Do your daily activities affect your lifespan?"

"Yes, my daily activities have a major effect on the aging process. Yoga, exercise, meditation, and relaxation are part of my daily activities, and they may help me live a longer life."

"Any activity that affects your sensations?"

"Using a smart phone is one of my major activities. I can't perform this activity without experiencing sensations like touch, sight, and hearing."

"Any activity that involves very little physical action?"

"The intensity of the physical action of my body, vocal organs, and mind is greatly reduced in the activity of meditation."

"Very well done, Jason. Living matter of the body has many physiological properties, but only four types of physiological properties are relevant to our quest. Physiological properties are manifested in the form of various vital functions of the physiology of living beings. The four relevant types of physiological properties are: 1. Sense property—controls the physical sensations of touch, taste, smell, vision, and hearing; 2. Power property—controls the physical actions of body, vocal organs, and mind; 3. Lifespan property—controls duration of embodiment; and 4. Physique[1] property—controls the development and upkeep of the body. Notice there are five subtypes of the sense property and three subtypes of power property. Though all living beings have lifespan and physique properties, they do not all have the same number of subtypes of sense and power properties. How many subtypes of sense and power properties do you have?"

"I believe I have all five subtypes of sense property and all three subtypes of power property."

"Correct. Here are some examples of living beings that don't have every subtype. Plants have only one subtype each of sense and power properties, namely, sense of touch and power of body. The number of subtypes of sense property of various insects and reptiles ranges between two and four, and all of them have two subtypes of power properties—power of body and power of vocal organs. However, human beings, birds, and mammals have all five subtypes of sense and three subtypes of power properties."

"I'm a little confused. Can you explain to me the distinction between power and physique properties?" I ask.

"Power property involves physical actions of body, vocal organs, and mind. Physique property involves development and maintenance of organs and various systems of the body, such as circulation, digestion, and respiration. This includes development and maintenance of the body, vocal organs, and mind, which become the means of physical actions. Does that make sense to you?"

"Yes, but then what do you mean by a lifespan property?"

"The lifespan property is related to the period of time during which the matter of the body of living beings continues to live. At the end of that period, a living being dies, and the body loses association with the soul at its departure from the body. The living matter of that body transforms into nonliving matter. In other words, the property of lifespan determines the length of life of a living being. Is that clear?"

"Yes, now I understand the concept of the lifespan property."

Guru continues, "There is more to understand about the sense and power properties. Senses have a hierarchy, starting from touch, at the most basic level, then taste, smell, vision, and hearing. Similarly, physical powers have a hierarchy, starting from the power of body then power of vocal-organs and finally power of mind. One-sensed living beings like plants have only one subtype of sense of touch and one subtype of power of body. Two-sensed living beings like worms, shells, and leeches have only two subtypes of senses of touch and taste and two subtypes of powers of body and vocal organs. Three-sensed living beings like bugs and ants have only three subtypes of senses of touch, taste, and smell and two subtypes of powers of body and vocal organs. Four-sensed living beings like reptiles, bees, and flies have four subtypes of senses of touch, taste, smell, and vision and two subtypes of powers of body and vocal organs. Five-living beings like humans, animals, birds, and fish have all five senses and all three powers. Only five-sensed living beings have power of mind. This knowledge of hierarchies of senses and means of physical actions will be used later in classifying different lifeforms. Any questions?"

"I'm not following this. A blind person doesn't have vision, but he can hear."

"The blind person has the sense of vision, but it is defective. Your 'to be discovered' karmic model will explain the reason of defective senses."

"Are there more extrinsic properties of matter besides these physiological properties?"

"Yes. We will discuss one more extrinsic property of living matter, but later when we talk about karmic matter. Let us move to the properties of soul now. I advise that you take a deep breath and relax."

I try to relax as suggested by Guru and mumble "Oh," as I make myself ready for a lesson in philosophy.

"Did you say something?" asks Guru.

I shake my head to answer no. Guru continues, "Tell me what you learned about soul on the Internet."

I open another folder on my laptop and read, "The soul, according to many religious and philosophic traditions, is the self-aware essence unique to living beings. In these traditions the soul is thought to incorporate the inner essence of each living being. Souls are presupposed to be immortal. The concept of the soul has strong links with notions of an afterlife, but opinions may vary widely, even within a given religion, as to what may happen to the soul after the death of living beings. These religions and philosophies see the soul as nonmaterial."

"Do you agree with what you just read?" asks Guru.

"Yes."

"Soul has numerous properties but let us try to comprehend the properties of soul that are most relevant to our quest. These properties of soul can be identified with the three faculties of consciousness—cognition, conation, and affection—recognized by psychologists. Do you remember that we discussed the faculties of consciousness yesterday?"

"Yes, I do."

"Jason, one property of soul—knowledge[2]—relates to cognition. The knowledge of the wild dog in the illustration you presented yesterday is the aspect of cognition. Can you identify another property of soul in your story which concerns the faculty of conation?"

"Before I answer your question, I'm confused about

something again. Would you help me a little more with the distinction between the power property of mind and the knowledge property of soul?"

"The property of knowledge of soul is described from an ontological viewpoint. The description of the property of knowledge is valid for all living beings ranging from one-sensed to five-sensed living beings. Living beings use five types of senses and three types of power of body, vocal organs, and mind to gain knowledge. Let us apply the concept of knowledge to a living plant that has only one sense of touch and one subtype of power of body. Using the information stored in its genetic body, the plant locates water with the help of its sense of touch and spreads its tentacles with the help of the body power. But this information alone is not sufficient to spread its tentacles in water. For that the plant needs the experience that it requires water for survival. Information combined with experience results in knowledge. In other words, experiential information results in knowledge. For humans, five types of senses and three types of power of body, vocal, organs, and mind deal with information that, combined with human experience, results in human knowledge.

"For living beings with mind, thinking is a physical process of managing and regulating information, which is possible only by mind activity, and the property of knowledge of soul plays no role in thinking. Of course, there would be no mind activity unless the nonliving matter had associated with soul to become living matter, however. Does this make sense to you, Jason?"

"Yes, I think so. Let me try to answer your earlier question about the property of soul which relates to the faculty of conation. Unfortunately, my answer is that I don't know what that property is."

"Let me help you, Jason. The property of soul relating to conation involves the volition to perform actions, e.g., the action of controlling one's desires. You should be able to grasp it if you answer the following question. We all have many desires, and we all try to control one or the other desire from time to time. How does one control one's desire?"

"I believe that we use our willpower to control desires."

"What do you mean by willpower? Do you mean one has to have physical power?"

"No, I don't think it's physical power. A physically weak person may be more capable of controlling his or her desire than a physically powerful person."

"You are right. Willpower is a metaphysical effort the nature of which is very different from that of physical effort. If willpower is not a physical power resulting from the body, then it must be a power of the soul. In other words, one needs spiritual power to control one's desires. Spiritual power is a property of soul, within the faculty of conation. The resolution of climbing the tree in the illustration is due to the property of spiritual power. Another property of soul concerns the faculty of affection, which deals with emotions caused by desires. Can you identify that property?"

"You'll have to help me with that, too."

"The property of soul related to the faculty of affection can be identified by thinking about the root cause of human desire, which is a false belief of oneness between soul and body. Humans generally do not differentiate between the soul and the body and have a misconception that 'I' am the body. Due to this false sense of self, which we will call ego, human beings develop desires for all things concerned with their body and remain engrossed in attachment to worldly objects and gratification of the senses. Desires lead to attachment and aversion that in turn create negative passions and negative quasi-passions.

"There are four negative passions: anger, pride, deceit, and greed; and nine negative quasi-passions: gaiety, pleasure, displeasure, grief, fear, disgust, and sexual cravings of three types: male, female, and hermaphrodite. We will see how these come into play later."

"And will you tell me why you are distinguishing between 'passions' and 'quasi-passions?'" I ask because I see that this question is going to distract me unless I know you are going to answer it at some point.

"Yes, Jason, I will get back to that question, trust me.

"Ego, passions, and quasi-passions are the constituents of a primary extrinsic property of soul, termed *moha* (delusion). Distortion due to ego is the fundamental constituent of *moha*; more about ego later. Are you with me?"

"Yes. I think so."

"A pure soul is devoid of *moha*, which is an impurity and an extrinsic property of soul, as the soul can exist without *moha*. *Moha* defiles an intrinsic property of soul, termed inner peace, consisting of true belief, equanimity, and contentment. True belief is demonstrated by a focus on soul, instead of body, as relevant to everlasting spiritual happiness.

"Equanimity presents a calm nature on all occasions, favorable as well as unfavorable. And contentment maintains self-containment. *Moha* and inner peace affect each other. As the intensity of the manifestation of *moha* decreases, the intensity of the manifestation of inner peace increases and vice versa. In a spiritually advanced human, inner peace is high and *moha* is low. Once the soul has become pure and left the worldly state, *moha* is shed. Can you name the properties of soul, which we just learned?"

"Yes. Soul has three intrinsic properties of knowledge, spiritual power, and inner peace and one extrinsic property of *moha*."

"Right. How do your daily activities affect the properties of your soul?"

"Well, it's obvious enough how knowledge is constantly affected by virtually everything I do. Let me think of examples for the other properties. One of my daily activities is attending to my finances, which involves shares in various stocks that my parents have given to me. I hate stocks that lose in value and love those that gain. The fluctuations in the stock market affect my *moha*, which in turn affects my inner peace."

"How do your daily activities affect your spiritual power?"

"The mode of spiritual power fluctuates wildly. Sometimes I have enough spiritual power to control my desires, while at other times I'm unable to do that. I don't know the cause of change in my spiritual power."

"You will find the cause once you discover the karma doctrine. So, save that thought for later."

Guru continues, "As we saw a hierarchy of physiological properties, there is also a hierarchy of soul properties. All living beings belong to one sentient class from a genus point of view, i.e., having feelings, cognition, and awareness, and all are identical from the soul's intrinsic properties point of view, i.e., having knowledge, spiritual power, and inner peace. Yet the manifestation of knowledge, spiritual power, and inner peace is not equal among them; in fact, this is the only major difference among them, in terms of soul. The manifestation of these properties in human beings is comparatively greater in degree. Among the animals and birds, it is lesser than human beings; in insects like ants and flies, less yet; among plants and trees, even less; and in microbes, it is still less. The manifestation of consciousness in microbes is so small that they cannot feel it. Are you with me?"

"Yes, but how do we know this?"

"The karmic model you are going to develop should be able to explain it."

"Okay, I will wait for it."

"Good. When a soul's properties attain the optimum state, it enters the status of a supreme being. In this way, every worldly soul possesses both the highest possibility of attaining the state of a supreme being but also the lowest possibility of becoming almost an inanimate substance, like a microbe or a bacterium.

When a worldly soul separates from matter, it develops into a pure soul and attains the state of a supreme being. A pure soul has perfect knowledge, unlimited spiritual power, and everlasting inner peace without *moha*. Any question, Jason?"

"I don't think so."

Guru takes a deep breath, and I sense that our time is up for the day. He says, "I am very pleased with your research activities and hope that you will keep it up."

"Thank you for the kind words," I say. But I am also glad that our session has come to an end, as there is so much to absorb and think about.

"Jason, I thank you for letting me continue our discussion beyond our scheduled time. You must be wondering when we will begin discussing the karma doctrine. I ask you to have patience for one more discussion. Tomorrow we will talk about causality. Understanding causality will help us grasp the karma doctrine, which is a law of cause and effect. If you have time, you can study it on the Internet."

"I will try my best to continue the research," I promise. And then I head for the library.

Notes

1. In Jainism "respiration," instead of "physique," is used as one of the physiological properties, as the capability of supporting the physique (body, senses, organs, and their appendages) is understood to be included within the capability of respiration.

2. In Jainism two properties of soul—perception and knowledge—are related to cognition. Consciousness is called "knowledge" when it is determinate and "perception" when it is indeterminate. Cognition includes both perception and knowledge. Both properties of soul are combined into one property of knowledge here to simplify the discussion.

Chapter 5

Causality

Today I am excited about my upcoming session on causality with Guru. I arrive at Guru's dwelling with my laptop, which includes a summary of the properties of matter and soul, plus my research on causality. We sit down as usual at the table, and I ask without wasting any time, "Should I present my summary of yesterday's discussion?"

Guru nods his head. I pull up my notes on the laptop and read out loud, "The metaphysical model of the karma doctrine is based on the basic presuppositions about the substances of matter and soul that we discussed two days ago and the following more detailed presuppositions:

1. Matter, both nonliving and living, has four intrinsic properties of touch, taste, odor, and color.
2. Living matter of the physical body has four extrinsic physiological properties — sense, power, lifespan, and physique. There are five subtypes of sense—touch, taste, smell, vision, and hearing; and three subtypes of power—physical actions of the body, vocal organs, and mind.
3. Soul has three intrinsic properties of knowledge, spiritual power, inner peace and one extrinsic property of *moha*."

"You have done an excellent job of summarizing the properties of soul and matter. Today we will explore the significance of causality, which implies that there must be a cause of everything happening in the universe."

"Are you saying, after all, that there must be a cause of the universe itself?"

"There is no cause of the universe itself as the constituents of the universe are eternal and uncreated. If you need a creator to create an eternal and uncreated substance, then you also need a creator of the creator. However, there is a cause of change in the state of the properties of the constituents."

"I will have to think about that."

"Let us hear what you learned about causality on the Internet."

I read, "Causality is defined as the relationship between one event or one mode of a substance (called cause) and another event or mode of the same substance (called effect) which is the consequence of the former."

"Can you explain the relationship between cause and effect through an example of events?"

"Sure. Consider the example where I fall while walking and injure myself. In this example there are two related events, which are: one, my falling; and the other, injuring myself. My falling is the cause of my injury, and my injury is the effect of my falling."

"What about an example using the modes of a substance?"

"Let's see. How about this? A piece of paper burns down by fire into ashes and fumes. This example involves two modes of matter; the old mode of matter before fire in the form of a piece of paper and the new mode of matter in the form of ashes and fumes. Fire is the cause of change in the mode of matter and the change in the mode of matter from a piece of paper to ashes and fumes is the effect of fire."

Guru says, "Let me present a different illustration. I make a cup out of a lump of clay using a potter's wheel and other tools. Can you identify the cause and the effect in this illustration?"

"Okay. You are the maker of the cup; hence you are the cause of the cup and the cup is the effect of your action of making pottery."

"Is it possible for me to make the cup without the potter's

wheel and other tools?"

"No, it's not possible to make the cup without them," I reply.

"Are they then the causes of the cup?"

"Yes, all of them, including you as the potter, are the causes of the cup."

"Is it possible for me to make the cup without the lump of clay?"

"No, you couldn't make the cup without the lump of clay."

"Is the lump of clay then also a cause of the cup?"

"I guess so."

"This example includes two modes of matter: the lump of clay and the cup of clay. These two modes of matter are related to each other. The lump of clay, or pre-mode of that matter, is a cause, and the cup of clay, or post-mode of that matter, is its effect. Now give an example which involves the modes of one of the properties of soul."

After a moment, I reply, "I can't think of such an example."

"Let me help you. Suppose you gain knowledge of a subject by attending a lecture given by a teacher. The mode of the property of knowledge of your soul changes by attending the lecture. Can you identify the cause of the change in the mode of your knowledge?"

"The lecture of the teacher is responsible for the change in the mode of my knowledge; hence the lecture is the cause and the change in my knowledge is the effect of my listening to the lecture."

"Suppose during the lecture you use some books that also help you in gaining the knowledge. Are then the books also the cause of the change in your knowledge?"

"Yes, books also are another cause of change in my knowledge."

"Let us examine the role of your knowledge prior to listening to the lecture. Was it possible for you to gain the knowledge without the knowledge you had before the lecture?"

"No, it wasn't possible."

"Are you saying that your knowledge prior to listening to the lecture also is responsible for gaining the knowledge?"

"Yes, that's what I'm saying."

"This example includes two modes of the property of knowledge of your soul: the mode before the lecture and the mode after the lecture. These two modes of knowledge are related to each other. The mode of knowledge of your soul before the lecture, i.e., the pre-mode of your soul, is a cause of the mode of knowledge of your soul after the lecture, i.e., the post-mode of your soul. The pre-mode of your soul is a cause of the post-mode of your soul, and the post-mode of your soul is the effect of the pre-mode of your soul. Are you with me?"

"I believe so."

"From these examples we can conclude that there can be more than one cause of change in the mode of a substance. For our discussion we will divide the causes into two kinds— material cause and efficient cause. The material cause is that which changes its own condition to bring about the effect. The effect is a potentiality in the material cause. The efficient cause is that which does not change its own condition to bring about the effect. The effect is nonexistent in the efficient cause. In the earlier illustration the lump of clay is the material cause, as the lump of clay changes itself to create the cup of clay. The lump of clay is no longer there once the cup is created. I, as a potter, the potter's wheel, and other tools are the efficient causes, as they do not change their own condition to create the cup of clay. I, as a potter, the potter's wheel, and other tools are still there after the creation of the cup. Do you understand the two types of causes?"

"Yes, I do, but I have a question. Why do you say that the lump of clay changes itself to create the cup? The lump of clay didn't really change into the cup of clay on its own; it was changed by you."

"A very intelligent question, Jason. All substances, including matter in the form of the lump of clay, have the potentiality of changing their mode continuously. Without the potentiality of always changing modes, the lump of clay could not be changed to the cup of clay. However, substances do not have the ability to decide their new mode. The new mode is governed by the efficient cause. The new mode of the lump of clay was controlled by me. Any question?"

"No."

"Then you should be able to identify in the example of soul the entities that function as one of the two kinds of causes. Can you do that?"

"Okay. In that example the mode of the soul before the lecture is the material cause as this mode of the soul changes itself into a different mode of the soul after the lecture. The lecture and the books are the efficient causes, as they do not change their own condition to produce the effect."

"Can you identify the material and efficient causes in the example where a piece of paper burns into ashes and fumes by fire?"

"The pre-mode of matter in the form of a piece of paper is the material cause; fire is the efficient cause; and the post-mode of matter in the form of ashes and fumes is the effect of burning the piece of paper by fire."

"Right! Let us go back to the example of the lump of clay. Was it possible for me to make a saucer from the lump of clay instead of the cup?"

"Yes, you could have made a saucer if you wanted."

"This means the lump of clay has the potentiality to change into different forms, such as a mug, bowl, or vase, which are different modes of matter. Now tell me whether the lump of clay has the knowledge of the possible forms."

"I don't think so."

"This means the lump of clay is not in a position to determine its next form. Who decides its next form?"

"The next form of the clay is decided by the potter."

"Let us apply this logic to your soul in the other example. Was it possible for you to do something different than attending the lecture?"

"Yes, I could have done millions of different things other than listening to the lecture."

"This means that the mode of your soul has the potentiality to change into any different mode out of the millions of them. Your soul has the capability to select its next mode. Such is not the case for the lump of clay. Do you see the difference in the process that controls the next mode in the animate and inanimate substances?"

"I do, and I understand the cause-effect relations. But I have one question. You just explained that my soul has the capability to select its next mode. What are the factors that govern the capability of my soul to select its next mode and who controls these factors?"

"A very intelligent question indeed, but you will have to wait for its answer, as it is embedded in the metaphysical model of the karma doctrine." Guru smiles at me, but I scratch my head. How much longer will I wait, I wonder.

He says, "I am very pleased with your progress. Your rate of learning is significantly higher than that of an average person. You should be able to discover the karma doctrine in a period shorter than I anticipated in the beginning."

These encouraging remarks help me live with my confusion and make me feel less impatient. I reply, "Thanks to you."

He continues, "We have completed the preliminaries of the karma doctrine. I am sure that you now have a better appreciation of them. The preliminaries have resulted in several presuppositions which will be indispensable in discovering the karma doctrine. Now tell me, why are you here?"

"I don't understand what you're saying," I reply. I feel

stunned right now. After all this work, all these mental gyrations over the last few days, is Guru trying to trick me?

"The answer to my question is trivial. You are here because you are composed of two uncreated and eternal substances. Your soul always exists in the universe. Your soul in the present embodiment is in the human lifeform. Does this make sense to you?"

"Yes," I say slowly. "It's true that 'I,' along with all living beings, am composed of the two eternal substances—soul and matter. And it's true that I, and all other beings alive at this moment, will not always exist in the form we are in now. So yes, the question 'Why am I here in the present form?' is, indeed, the most relevant question." As I say these words aloud, I realize that Guru has not tricked me—only helped me clarify my question.

"We know that the soul can exist either in the pure form or worldly form. We also know that our souls in the present form are worldly souls. What was the state of our souls before getting here in the present form? Were they worldly souls or pure souls?" asks Guru.

"I have no idea."

"We learned that the state of the pure soul is the supreme state of the soul. Every soul would like to attain that supreme state. It is logical to assume that a pure soul which has attained the supreme state will never transform back into a worldly soul and thus always stays in the supreme state. Because of this it is reasonable to assume that our soul in its previous lives was a worldly soul. In other words, a living being keeps taking rebirth until its worldly soul transforms into a pure soul. And reincarnation is a logical phenomenon. Do you agree?"

"Yes, but it doesn't explain to me why I'm a male human being in the present life or what form I'll have in my next life."

"You are correct. We need to discover the model of the karma doctrine that determines the form in the next life. We will begin discovering the model tomorrow. In the meantime, I will ask you to reflect upon the question yourself. Would you have time to also do some research?"

"Yes, just tell me the topic."

"The topic is universality, for which the Internet will again be most useful."

"I'll do that," I say. Surely, I am already increasing my spiritual power. Or am I just increasing my desire for spiritual power and thus increasing my unhappiness if I do not fulfill my desire? Oh well. At least for the time being I am full of excitement that soon all these abstract principles will lead to enlightenment. I head for the library before going back to camp to study.

Chapter 6

Actions and Consequences

Today we'll begin discovering the metaphysical model of the karma doctrine. With elation I arrive at the Guru's dwelling a little early, pondering the question of what principle determines a being's life-form in the next birth, but without any answer. I know Guru will ask me about it, and I'm afraid I'll look stupid if I say I have no answer. Guru looks at me as I take my regular seat and asks, "Did you ponder the functional aspects of the karma doctrine?"

"Yes, I did, but without much success."

"You tried, and that is good enough for me. It is a daunting task to discover the functional process of this doctrine. Are you ready to discover it?" asks Guru.

"As ready as I can be."

"We are going to be basing the metaphysical model of the karma doctrine on presuppositions that are related to the substances that constitute living beings, namely, soul and matter and their properties. We have already discussed these presuppositions which we should keep in mind as we will need them often. Let me hear these presuppositions from you."

I was prepared for such a question since it's the same thing we started with yesterday. "Living beings are made up of two uncreated and eternal substances—soul and matter. Matter has four intrinsic properties of touch, taste, odor, and color and four extrinsic physiological properties of sense, power, lifespan, and physique. Soul has three intrinsic properties of knowledge, spiritual power, and inner peace and one extrinsic property of *moha*."

"You have done an excellent job. I could not have done it better. It is imperative that we have unconditional faith in these presuppositions, as they form the foundation of the metaphysical model. If you have any disbelief in any of the presuppositions, you should speak now."

"I think I understand the presuppositions, but I don't have unconditional faith in them. It's my hope that I'll develop unconditional faith in them when I discover the model of the karma doctrine."

"Fair enough. I am sure you know that most religions preach that human beings should perform virtuous actions. What could be the basis for such a preaching?"

"I think virtuous actions serve everyone," I reply.

"Your premise is correct. This preaching is based on a metaphysical presupposition that virtuous actions give rise to favorable consequences. A corollary of this presupposition is that evil actions produce adverse consequences. This presupposition and its corollary are the basis of the karma doctrine. The doctrine asserts that living beings bear the consequences of their actions. Do you follow me?" inquires Guru.

"Yes, I understand this."

"Then tell me your understanding of consequences of actions."

"When a person performs an evil action, he or she gets punishment for it. The punishment is the consequence of his or her evil action. The incarceration one undergoes because of his or her action of theft is an example of a consequence as punishment," I reply.

"You are correct. Generally, the consequences are thought of as punishment only. But a consequence in this doctrine has a broader meaning; it includes both rewards and punishments. Can you give an example of an action that has a reward?"

"The remuneration a person receives for performing a job and the material goods they acquire using the remuneration would be examples of a consequence as reward."

"Good. Although almost all religions have referenced

a system of rewards and punishments for behavior, their explanations are either inadequate, or the explanations are not logically presented, or the premises do not lead to a consistent reply to every query. For example, many religions have circumvented the dilemma of understanding the system by leaving the administration of the system to God. In other words, God determines punishments and rewards. But the invocation of God for administering the system raises more questions than it answers. It fails to provide proper answers to questions as to why evil people live luxurious lifestyles, or why people vary so much in shape, size, income level, and physical health. Do you agree with me?"

"I personally prefer an explanation which doesn't invoke God. It's too easy to replace an inexplicable phenomenon with God, which itself is inexplicable," I respond.

"The only way to circumvent this dilemma is to discover a metaphysical model that provides the answers to these questions and a logical explanation of the system. You will discover such a model in our discourse. Let us first try to understand the nature of actions. How do you perform actions?"

"I perform actions with my body, vocal organs, and mind."

"Your answer is partially correct. All three means of physical activity—body, vocal organs, and mind—are made of living matter. Does your soul play any role in your actions?"

"I know what you're saying," I respond. "There's always a motivation behind each action, and the motivation stems from the soul. So, my soul plays a role in my actions."

"The karma doctrine deals with intentional, voluntary actions that include two components: physical actions of the body, vocal organs, and mind, termed *yoga*; and psychic activity that involves intentions, motivations, desires, etc., which in turn is steered by *moha*. In short, an action is an activity performed by *yoga*-plus-*moha*."

"I'm confused. I thought that *yoga* meant a system of physical exercises."

"You are correct, but the term *yoga* has been defined in several ways. We will use the definition given in a 2nd-century CE Jain text wherein the term *yoga* is defined as the sum of all the actions of mind, vocal organs, and body."

I take a moment to digest this new information. My brain almost hurts with these additional words! I simply repeat *yoga* and *moha,* hoping that they will stick in some corner of my mind.

Guru continues, "Tell me what you learned about universality on the Internet?"

I locate the file on my laptop and read confidently, "A proposition is considered universal if it is valid in all times and at all places. For example, the law of gravity is a universal law, because it's valid everywhere in the universe and at all times."

"Knowing the meaning of universality, let us try to understand the characteristics of the karma doctrine. Is this doctrine valid everywhere in the universe?"

"I think so. The karma doctrine would become meaningless if it was applicable only at some places and not at other places. For example, if it's assumed that the karma doctrine is applicable only in India and not in other countries, then a person could make the karma doctrine meaningless by performing desirable actions in India and undesirable actions in other countries. The karma doctrine should be applicable to all living beings, irrespective of their location in the universe. It should, therefore, be valid everywhere in the universe where living beings reside," I reply.

"Right again! Is the karma doctrine valid all the time?"

"Again, the karma doctrine would become meaningless if it isn't applicable at all times. For example, if it's assumed that the karma doctrine is applicable only on weekends and not on weekdays, then a person could make the karma doctrine meaningless by performing desirable actions on weekends and undesirable action on weekdays. Living beings perform actions all the time, so the doctrine would be meaningless if it's applicable only part of the time. Therefore, I think the doctrine should be valid all the time."

"Correct again! Can we then conclude that the karma doctrine must be a universal doctrine?"

"Yes. The doctrine must be valid everywhere and at all times, a universal doctrine," I respond.

"If the karma doctrine is to be universal, then the laws that govern the relationships between actions and their consequences also should be universal. The consequences of an action should depend only on the action, not on the time and place of the action. Whether the action is performed in the U.S. or in India, or somewhere else in the universe, the karma-doctrine-governed consequences of that action must be identical. Likewise, whether an action was performed in the past, or is performed today, or will be performed in the future, the karma-doctrine-governed consequences of that action must be identical. Are you with me?"

"It makes sense to me."

"Must karma-doctrine-governed consequences of actions be universal?"

"Based on what you just said, the karma-doctrine-governed consequences of an action must depend only on the action, not the place and the time of the action. The karma-doctrine-governed consequences are, therefore, universal."

"From here on I will refer to the universal karma-doctrine-governed consequences simply as universal consequences. Is that okay?"

"Yes."

"Let us go back to consequences in the form of reward and punishment. Are the remunerations for a particular job or the duration of incarceration for theft in different countries identical?"

"No, they aren't the same in different countries."

"Does the remuneration for a particular job or the duration of incarceration for a particular crime vary with time? Was it different in the past than the present and will it be different in the future?"

"Definitely."

"These two consequences, remuneration and imprisonment, vary with time and place of actions. They cannot, therefore, be universal consequences. Such consequences are non-universal. Do you agree?"

"Yes, but I never thought about them in this way."

"Do not be disheartened. You are not alone. Most people think the same way. How are the non-universal consequences of actions governed?"

"I know the two consequences in your example, remuneration and imprisonment, are governed by human-made laws that are non-universal, because they change with time and place."

"The non-universal consequences of actions are governed by factors, including human-made laws, that change with time and place. We will call these environmental factors. In other words, environmental-factor-governed consequences, which I will refer to from now on simply as environmental consequences, are non-universal, because they change with time and place. This finding can be used to formulate a rule for determining universal and environmental consequences. The rule is: the consequences of an action that are not controlled by environmental factors are universal consequences, which are governed by the karma doctrine. And the consequences of an action that are controlled by environmental factors are environmental consequences, which are non-universal. Does this make sense, Jason?"

"I had the misunderstanding that all consequences of actions are governed by the karma doctrine, while the reality is that only universal consequences are governed by the karma doctrine."

"It is important to realize that every action has universal consequences. Both actions discussed earlier, performing a job and committing theft, have environmental, as well as universal, consequences. But not every action needs to have environmental consequences, as explained by the example I am about to present. A man spends several days secretly planning the murder of an enemy but fails to do so because the enemy disappeared from the region. What kind of consequences of his action of planning the murder do you think he will experience?"

"Only that person, nobody else, knows that he spent several days planning the murder. Unless he confesses his crime, he isn't going to experience any environmental consequences, but he can't escape from bearing the universal consequences."

"Very good, Jason! Most people, sometime in their lives, have thought about committing various kinds of evils. They believe that such thoughts have no consequences. But this conclusion is flawed. Though such actions have no environmental consequences, they do have universal consequences that they will have to bear in the future."

Now I have the answer to the question raised in my discussion with Ajay a few months back, when he advised me to contact the Guru: why did the two thieves have different consequences even though both committed the same action of theft? The thief who wasn't caught by the police became rich, while the other thief, who was caught by the police, was incarcerated. The consequences of the same action of theft were different because such environmental consequences aren't governed by the universal karma doctrine. They are controlled by non-universal environmental factors. The capture of one thief and not the other by the police is controlled by circumstances, and the incarceration is governed by human-made laws. Both circumstances and human-made laws are elements of non-universal environmental factors. But both thieves have universal consequences that they will have to bear in the future.

Guru continues, "The importance of distinguishing between universal and environmental consequences cannot be overemphasized. There is a prevailing erroneous notion that the karmic doctrine was created by the ruling elites to maintain control over the down-trodden segment of society. However, that notion was based on the assumption that environmental consequences are governed by karmic doctrine, which we see is not true. Only universal consequences, that apply to rich and poor alike, are governed by karmic doctrine. Any questions, Jason?"

"Though I can identify environmental consequences, I can't say the same for universal consequences. I need your help in understanding what they are."

"Universal consequences are invisible to our senses. We must, therefore, take a different approach to understand them. A few days ago, we studied the properties of matter and soul to prepare to understand how universal consequences affect the modes of these properties. To appreciate universal consequences, we need to understand the process by which they affect the modes of the properties of soul and body. We can get some clue from science's explanation of the function of DNA molecules. We will continue our discussion Monday. In the meantime, you could read about DNA and dark matter/dark energy on the Internet."

I bow my head to Guru and leave for the library to study about dark matter and dark energy. I don't need to read about DNA. I already know about it from my biology class. It doesn't take long to read about dark matter and dark energy. I then leave for the camp site while trying to form an idea of the nature of universal consequences.

Chapter 7

Karmic Body

The sky is cloudy this Friday night as I can watch it through the screen of my tent while lying inside. I'm feeling more relaxed tonight because there is no discourse with Guru on the weekend. I know that hiking is the only true way to enjoy the natural beauty of the Yellowstone.

Saturday morning I hike on Storm Point Loop Trail to get the grand view of forest, beach, and waterfall in one hike. Sunday I hike on Uncle Tom's Trail that carries you from the top of the Grand Canyon of the Yellowstone to the base of the 308-foot lower Falls where you get the iconic Yellowstone view of the water falls. The weekend hiking energizes me for the weekday's discourses.

On Monday I arrive at the Guru's dwelling. Universal consequences have been on my mind since Friday. As soon as I take my regular seat, Guru asks me, "Can you give me an example of a universal consequence?"

"I have been thinking about it, but I can't come up with anything."

"How can you have faith in the karma doctrine if you cannot identify even one universal consequence?" Guru smiles at me. I know his reprimand is gentle and meant to be humorous. "Now you know why you do not have unconditional faith in the karma doctrine. Your current understanding of universal consequences is not in accordance with the karma doctrine. Let us start to modify that. We perform actions all the time, and we also receive, concurrently, directives for the universal consequences of these actions. What do you think of that?" asks Guru.

"I'm a little confused. Are you saying that I'm receiving

directives for the universal consequences of my actions right this moment? But I can't think of any directives that I'm receiving at present. Can you explain what a directive is?"

"You can think of a directive like a bit of code that provides instructions for the execution of universal consequences associated with a particular action, based on the law of the karma doctrine. We will be studying this more in a bit. Yes, I am saying that you are receiving these directives right at this moment," responds Guru.

"But I still can't comprehend the nature of the consequences you're talking about."

"You are going to have to be patient as you gain that comprehension over the course of our conversation today. Keep in mind I am talking strictly about the universal consequences of actions, not environmental consequences. We receive the directives for these universal consequences all the time. These directives are stored in a carrier for execution in the future. However, we are unable to perceive the nature of universal consequences head-on because the carrier of their directives is invisible to our senses and available scientific tools. Do you remember the process of universal consequences that we learned Friday?"

"Yes. Universal consequences affect the modes of the properties of soul and body."

"There is actually a time gap between the two events of receiving directives and changing the modes of the properties of soul and body through universal consequences. There is a need to store the directives somewhere. Moreover, it is possible that some universal consequences are not experienced in the present life but are borne into the next life. Therefore, there is a need to identify a carrier that conveys, to the next life, the stored directives for the universal consequences of actions performed in the present life. Do you have any idea where the directives are stored?"

"I know that a lot of information can be stored on a tiny memory chip, but I don't think I carry a memory chip inside my body."

"You are right in thinking that there is no memory chip inside our bodies, like a memory chip inside processor units of computers. But you will see that our bodies do carry a sort of 'memory chip' that is made of subtle matter.[1] The soul leaves the body at the time of death of the living being and passes into another physical body in the next life. This process is called transmigration of the soul. The phenomenon of the transmigrating soul inhabiting a new physical body in the next life is called rebirth, which is a necessary corollary of the karma doctrine. The transmigrating soul is a worldly soul which, according to the karma doctrine, still has association with a type of matter. However, we are unable to perceive the transmigrating soul, or the matter associated with it by means of our senses and available scientific tools. This implies that matter associated with the transmigrating worldly soul must be in the form of subtle matter. What could be the purpose of the association of subtle matter with soul?"

"I have no clue. I wouldn't have ever guessed that there is subtle matter involved."

"That is why one needs a teacher for guidance when one's intuition fails. Let us approach it this way. What did you learn about DNA on the Internet?"

"I didn't need to look it up on the Internet because I remember it from my biology course in high school."

"Do you remember the function of DNA molecules?" asks Guru.

"The main role of DNA molecules is the long-term storage of biological information. DNA molecules have the power to deliver the genetic instructions needed to construct components of the body's cells, such as protein and RNA molecules."

"That's right. If DNA molecules have such a power, it

seems logical to assume that subtle matter in association with a worldly soul has the capability to deliver the directives for universal consequences. The metaphysical model of the karma doctrine is based on the presupposition that subtle matter, called karmic matter, is the carrier of directives for the universal consequences of actions. Karmic matter makes up the karmic body that worldly souls always carry with them, even during transmigration. All living beings must have a karmic body. Now we need one more element, which will help us in developing the model."

Guru sighs deeply. He does this occasionally, and that's when I recognize that these intellectual exercises in logic are difficult for him too. But knowing there's just one more element gives me hope and seems to energize him too, because he seems to lighten up as he asks, "What could be the source of karmic matter?"

"This must be where my study of dark matter and dark energy on the Internet comes into play. Scientists believe that what appears to be empty space in the universe is filled entirely with dark matter/dark energy, which isn't directly visible or detectable by current scientific instruments. This sounds very much like your definition of subtle matter. If this belief is true, then it does seem possible to presuppose that a portion of the dark matter that fills the space in the universe is karmic matter."

"Excellent observation, Jason. In metaphysics we use the term subtle matter, instead of dark matter. A portion of dark/subtle matter in the universe may be massless, as scientists are not definite about the nature of dark matter. We will assume the karmic body is massless, since the worldly soul could not carry a karmic body with mass during transmigration. A question then arises. How does karmic matter become associated with the soul? Do you have any idea?"

"No idea," I reply.

"Karmic particles (basic elements of karmic matter) are

much finer than the body cells of living beings. They easily penetrate the body through the spaces between cells, wherein they become associated with the soul and transform into living karmic matter. The living karmic matter of the karmic body will be called karma. Every action of a living being binds karma to its karmic body. And karma serves as a carrier and a deliverer of the directives for universal consequences of actions. These consequences manifest in the form of the modes of the properties of the soul and living matter of the body. Can you infer the domain of influence of the karmic body?"

"I know that the domain of influence of genetics is confined within the individual physical body. If I understand correctly, karma is a cause of modification of pre-modes to post-modes of the properties of the individual soul and body. In that case, it seems logical to infer that the effect of the karmic body should remain confined to the individual soul and body."

"Jason, I am impressed with your answer. Karma does not cause events outside the physical body, and it cannot affect environmental factors, such as one's material wealth and social status." Guru stares at me and says, "It seems from your facial expressions that you want to say something to me?"

"I was under the impression that one's material wealth and social status are controlled by one's karma."

"You are not alone; most people have that impression. The word 'karma' has multiple definitions in general use, including actions and fate/destiny. Our actions and environmental factors do control our wealth and social status. However, I deliberately avoided using the word 'karma' for actions to prevent confusion with this misunderstanding. More accurately, the word 'karma' means the living karmic matter that is bound to the karmic body and functions as the carrier and deliverer of the directives for universal consequences of actions. Material wealth and social status are not universal consequences and, therefore, not governed by the karma doctrine. They are controlled by environmental factors that include circumstances and human-made laws."

"Are you saying that the question of why some bad people have good experiences of wealth and prestige while some good people have bad experiences of poverty and disgrace cannot be answered using the karma doctrine?"

"I could not have said it better."

"I'll have to be careful how I use the word 'karma' in the future." I'm clearer now what universal consequences are not, but I still don't know what they are. I know I have to be patient.

"Similar to the living matter of a physical body acquiring extrinsic physiological properties, the living matter of the karmic body also acquires extrinsic properties. Bondage, which is the state of binding the karmic matter to the karmic body, is one of the extrinsic properties of the karmic body. Bondage deals with the amount of karmic matter bound to the karmic body, the number and types of karma, the time of fruition of karma, and the intensity of consequences of karma. We will be talking about bondage during our remaining discussion time today. We need these details of bondage to boost your faith in the karma doctrine. Do you know what controls the amount of karmic matter bound to the karmic body?"

"I don't have the faintest idea."

"In karmic doctrine we presuppose that the karmic body pulsates incessantly, just like body cells do. The amount of karmic matter attached to the karmic body with an action depends on the intensity of pulsation of the karmic body during the action. That intensity of pulsation of the karmic body is in turn modulated by the physical actions of living beings, i.e., *yoga*. Remember physical actions can be bodily, vocal or mental. *Yoga* is in turn affected by the degree of *moha* with which the physical action is carried out. For example, during meditation *moha* tends to be low, as do physical, vocal and mental activity. The pulsation of the karmic body during meditation would, therefore, be mild, and the amount of karmic matter attached to the karmic body during meditation would be small. On the other hand, as the pulsation of the karmic body would be intense during rage and agitation, the amount of karmic matter attached to the karmic body would be large. Thus, the amount of karmic matter bound to the karmic body during an action increases with the intensity of *moha* with which the action is carried out. Any questions?"

"No."

"How many types of karma do you think there are in the karma doctrine?"

"I'd guess that the number of types of karma should depend on the number of properties of soul and body. The soul has three intrinsic properties of knowledge, spiritual power, and inner peace and one extrinsic property of *moha*. There should, therefore, be four types of karma that affect the properties of soul. And the body has four intrinsic properties of touch, taste, odor, and color and four extrinsic physiological properties of sense, power, lifespan, and physique. The types of karma that affect the properties of body should, therefore, be eight. Am I right?"

"Your answer is partly correct. As *moha* and inner peace are mutually dependent properties of soul, one type of karma affects both properties. There are, therefore, three types of karma that affect the properties of soul. Moreover, the intrinsic properties of matter that you mention are perceived by the sense organs, which are included in the physique physiological property. Therefore, we do not need to count the four intrinsic properties separately. Thus, there are only four main types of karma that affect the four physiological properties of living matter—sense, power, lifespan, and physique. Is that clear?"

"Yes. Now I understand that there are only seven types of karma—three affect the properties of soul, and the remaining four affect the properties of living matter of the body. But I have a question. How does karma get transformed into seven types to carry different universal consequences?"

"It is not as difficult to understand as you think. Tell me what happens to the piece of bread you eat every day."

"It gets transformed into different constituents of my body," I reply.

"Very good, Jason. Does the piece of bread have prior knowledge about the transformation?"

"No. The piece of bread is inanimate and therefore has no knowledge of transformation."

"So, the piece of bread, upon association with the soul, acquires the capability to transform into different constituents of the body. Similarly, karma is inanimate, but upon associating with the soul, acquires the capability to transform into seven main types and numerous subtypes. Does this make sense?" asks Guru.

"It does."

"We need to discuss the remaining two aspects of bondage: time and intensity of consequences. Karma has the capability to remain attached to the karmic body for a varying length of time before detaching from it at fruition. This is called duration bondage. And the capability of fruition is called fruition bondage. Both capabilities are dictated by the intensity of *moha* at the time of the original actions. The time of fruition of karma can range from a few instants to countless years, depending on the intensity of *moha*. Can you come up with logic to relate the time of fruition to the intensity of *moha*?"

"Not without your help."

"The main purpose of our life as human beings is to transform our worldly soul to a pure soul, termed liberation, by detaching karma from the karmic body. The longer karma remains bound to the soul, the more delayed is its time of becoming a pure soul. If one person performs action with intense *moha* and the other person with mild *moha*, whose soul should achieve liberation in less time?"

"You taught me that *moha* is impurity of the soul. Therefore, the more intense the impurity, it seems the longer the time should be to achieve liberation. The time of fruition, therefore, should increase as the intensity of *moha* increases and vice versa."

"Brilliant! Can you now develop a similar logic for the intensity of consequences of karma?"

"Okay. Let me try explaining it using an illustration. Suppose a person performs an evil action and the universal consequence of the evil action is that he or she will experience pain in the future. I think the intensity of pain should depend on the intensity of *moha* with which the evil action was carried out. The intensity of pain should increase with increased intensity of *moha*. Therefore, the intensity of consequences of karma would increase with the intensity of *moha* with which the actions were carried out and vice versa."

"Jason, you always surprise me with your marvelous performance in grasping the fundamentals of the karma doctrine. I am sure you now understand that the question why some evil people have favorable experiences of wealth and prestige while some good people have unfavorable experiences of poverty and disgrace cannot be answered with the karma doctrine. Right?"

I'm humbled by the Guru's remarks and respond, "Wealth, poverty, prestige, and disgrace are environmental consequences that aren't governed by the karma doctrine. That question can't, therefore, be answered with the karma doctrine."

"Well said. We now have the basic ideas of the elements of the karma doctrine system. Those elements are actions and their universal consequences and karma. An outline of the system can be predicated upon using the elements of the system. Actions attach karma to the karmic body. Karma contains directives for delivering the universal consequences of actions. Karma remains inactive for a time period determined by *moha*. Karma then becomes active, delivers the universal consequences, and detaches from the soul. The universal consequences affect the modes of the properties of soul and living matter of the body, including the modes of the actions of living beings. New actions attach new karma to the karmic body and the cycle continues. Do you follow me?" asks Guru.

"Yes. I can even see some similarity between this system and new ideas emerging in scientific publications, that the soul and the body affect each other. I'm impatient to learn the details of the system."

"We will study the details in our future discourses. Though we have introduced seven types of karma, we have not yet discussed their nature and function. We also have not discussed other extrinsic properties of the karmic body besides bondage. Soon we will deal with them, including examples of how karma manifests in one's life, because we do not have enough time left today to complete that discussion."

"But before we conclude today's session, I want to emphasize that the properties of soul and living matter of the body are universal, since they do not change with time and place; and the modes of these universal properties are controlled by the universal consequences of actions. Thus, universal consequences become the cause of changes in the modes of properties of the soul and body. Therefore, both the cause and the effect are universal."

"It makes sense to me that a universal cause has a universal effect."

"Jason, excellent job. Tomorrow we will explore the details of karma. Keep pondering the nature of karma."

I bow my head and leave for the campsite, but I'm clueless about how to ponder the new information.

Notes

1. In metaphysics the term "subtle matter" refers to the fact that it is too fine to be detected using available scientific equipment.

Chapter 8

Karma

Late into the night I think about universal consequences, karma, and the karma doctrine in a way that begins to make sense to me. I'm excited to learn the nature and function of various types of karma. I arrive at the Guru's dwelling with this excitement.

Guru stares at me as if he's trying to read my mind. As I take my seat, he remarks, "It looks to me like you are eager to learn the details of karma."

I smile and say, "You're right!"

"Karma carries a specific connotation in the karma doctrine. Do you remember what it is?"

"Karma is the karmic matter that's bound to the karmic body and carries and delivers the universal consequences of actions."

"Very good, Jason. Always keep this meaning of karma in your mind; never muddle it up with actions and fate/destiny."

"I'll be careful."

"As I will frequently use the term 'karmic debt' in our discourse, I must define this term. Karmic matter attached to the karmic body is understood as debt to be liquidated in the future and is termed karmic debt. The karmic body can be thought of as an individual bank account where the ledger of the karmic debt of the individual is kept. Since *moha* is the cause of bondage of karma to the karmic body, the karmic debt incurred during an action depends on the intensity of the *moha* associated with the action. The larger the intensity of *moha* with which the action is carried out, the larger is the karmic debt acquired during that action. As we constantly acquire and liquidate karmic debt, the total karmic debt in an individual bank account constantly keeps changing. If you have any questions about this term, you must ask now."

"I think I understand the meaning of the term karmic debt."

"Well, then, let us talk about karma. Karma is divided into two groups—psychical karma and physiological karma—based on its influence on the properties of soul and body. Each karma carries a different universal consequence that in turn affects the different properties of soul and body. Do you remember the properties of soul?"

"Yes. The three intrinsic properties of soul are knowledge, spiritual power, and inner peace and the one extrinsic property of soul is *moha*."

"There are three psychical karmas that affect the properties of soul you just mentioned. Two of the three psychical karmas are the knowledge-obscuring[1] and spiritual-power-obscuring karmas. Fruition of these karmas, i.e., delivery of karmic consequences by these karmas, prevents manifestation of perfect knowledge and unlimited spiritual power of the worldly soul in living beings. These karmas do not destroy, but only obstruct, the inherent knowledge and spiritual power of soul, so that only partial knowledge and spiritual power manifest in worldly souls. You might think of it like how clouds obstruct, but do not destroy, solar energy. Can you guess the third psychical karma?"

"I think it must be related to the properties of *moha* and inner peace of the soul."

"You are correct, Jason. The third psychical karma is the nature-deluding karma that partly defiles the property of inner peace of soul with *moha*, which is an impurity of soul. As the intensity of manifestation of the nature-deluding karma increases, the intensity of manifestation of inner peace decreases and the intensity of manifestation of *moha* increases. Partial defilement of the property of inner peace with *moha* lies at the very heart of karmic bondage. Are you with me?"

"I believe so. I now understand that *moha* and inner peace are not independent properties of soul, as both are affected simultaneously by one karma, i.e., the nature-deluding karma."

"We need to remind ourselves of the three constituents of the property of *moha*. Can you recall them?"

"I believe they are ego, negative passions and quasi-passions."

"Always keep these three constituents in mind. Let us go back to physiological karma. There are four types of physiological karma that affect the four types of physiological properties of living matter. One of them is the feeling-determining karma that deals with the sense property. Fruition of this karma affects the performance of senses and is responsible for worldly experiences of misery and pleasure. Do you understand, Jason?"

"Shouldn't it be called sensation-determining karma, instead of feeling-determining karma?"

"You have a valid argument, Jason. Sensations have the capability of physical sensation only, not the capability of discriminating between misery and pleasure. However, nature-deluding karma does have this capability. Feeling-determining karma is the only karma among the seven types of karma that always functions together with nature-deluding karma. As a result, feeling-determining karma, in conjunction with nature-deluding karma, is responsible for the experience of misery and pleasure. Does that answer your question?"

"Yes, it makes sense to me now."

"The other three types of physiological karma are power-, lifespan-, and physique-determining karma. Power-determining karma deals with the power property. Fruition of this karma affects bodily movements, vocal expressions, and mental choices. Lifespan-determining karma deals with the lifespan property. This karma determines the duration of embodiment. Physique-determining karma deals with the physique property. This karma has a variety of functions ranging from determining the realm of birth to the minutest details of the body. Do you have any questions related to the main types of karma?"

"Can you give some examples of the realm of birth?"

"Yes, these include plant, insect, animal, human, etc."

"So, my physique-determining karma determines the type of living being I'll be in my next reincarnation?" I ask.

"That is correct. One subtype of the physique-determining karma does determine lifeform in the next reincarnation. Any more questions?"

"I understand that there are karmic consequences, but what causes them?"

"Jason, before I answer your question tell me what you mean by karmic consequences."

"Here's how I understand it. Karma, at the end of its bondage duration, detaches from the karmic body, delivers its universal consequences of past actions in the form of karmic consequences that manifest as new modes of the properties of soul and body, and then transforms into nonliving karmic matter."

"Well said, Jason. Are karmic consequences possible without fruition of karma?"

"I don't think so."

"So, you have the answer to your question; fruition of karma is the cause of karmic consequences."

"Are you saying that the change in the mode of the property of knowledge of my soul during our discussion on the karma doctrine is determined by fruition of the knowledge-obscuring karma of my past actions?"

"That is correct."

"Does this mean that you aren't playing any role in changing the mode of my knowledge?"

"What do you think?"

"The change in my knowledge of the karma doctrine isn't possible without your counseling. So, your role of counseling is also a cause of change in my knowledge."

"Let us analyze your response. You are currently performing the action of listening to me. Means are required to perform actions. Means involve substances, both living and nonliving, time, and region. For example, your current action of listening to me is not possible without me as a living substance, my dwelling as a nonliving substance and a region for counseling, and the time for listening. All these means, including me as your guide, are a subgroup of environmental factors, and are causes of change in your knowledge. Thus, there are two causes of karmic consequences; one cause is fruition of karma, and the second cause is environmental factors. Is that clear?"

"Yes."

"Can you identify the material and efficient causes of karmic consequences?"

"Fruition of karma is the material cause, and the environmental factors are the efficient cause."

"Are both causes governed by the karma doctrine?"

"I don't think that my meeting with you in your dwelling now has any causal relationship with karma from my past actions. The efficient cause—the environmental factors—isn't governed by the karma doctrine. Of course, the material cause—fruition of karma—is governed by the karma doctrine."

"Are you saying that we were not destined to meet here now?"

"Yes! That's what I'm saying. If the environmental factors are not governed by the karma doctrine, how could it predestine our meeting?"

"Your logic is correct, Jason. We are having the meeting because we have free will. We will discuss the topic of free will in detail later. Let us talk about fruition of another type of karma. Which karma do you think controls our health?"

"It must be one of the physiological karmas, because health concerns the body, not the soul. It has to be the physique-determining karma."

"If the physique-determining karma controls our health, then what is the role of a physician in the recovery of a patient?"

"I suppose the karmic consequence of the physique-determining karma has two causes—the material cause that is fruition of physique-determining karma and the efficient cause that includes the physician and other environmental factors. Karmic consequences will be different with different efficient causes. For example, the effect on the health of the patient will depend upon the capability of the physician and suitability of the environment. A talented physician and a more suitable environment can have a more desirable effect on the recovery of the patient."

"Can you give an example to illustrate the effect of the fruition of the physique-determining karma on the health of the patient, Jason?"

"You'll have to help me with that."

"One of the subtypes of the physique-determining karma is the immune-suppressing karma that controls the immune system. Can you project the effect of the intensity of consequences of the immune-suppressing karma on the health of the patient?"

"I suppose the milder the intensity of consequences of the immune-suppressing karma, the more desirable the effect is on the recovery of the patient."

"Very good, Jason. We will study one more example which involves the karmic consequences of the feeling-determining karma. Consider the case of a person who withstands a loss of property due to a natural disaster, and the loss of property makes him miserable. The feeling of misery is the karmic consequence of the feeling-determining karma, in conjunction with nature-deluding karma. What is the role of the natural disaster in the karmic consequence?"

"The natural disaster is the efficient cause of the misery."

"Is this efficient cause governed by the karma doctrine?"

"No, the natural disaster depends on environmental factors, which aren't controlled by the karma doctrine."

"Is the loss of property controlled by the karma doctrine?"

"Since a natural disaster is not controlled by the karma doctrine, neither is the loss of property."

"Though the main cause of karmic debt is *moha*, it takes the support of other factors to manifest itself. It is important to know these factors that impact the karmic debt, so that one can try to control them. I will explain these factors through several examples. First, let us consider this case in point. One person shoots a deer with an arrow intentionally, while another person unknowingly shoots a deer by mistake. Both persons perform the same physical action, but with different intentions. Who will amass the more karmic debt?"

"An action encompasses both physical action and intentions. It's logical to infer that the karmic debt will be more severe for the intentional killer than the unintentional killer."

"Right! Consider another example. Two persons watch the same drama in a theater: one, with mild attachment; and the other, with strong attachment. Is there going to be a difference in their karmic debt?"

"Yes. The greater the attachment, the greater the *moha*, and hence the karmic debt. The person who watches the drama with mild attachment will accumulate less karmic debt."

"Correct! In both examples, the two persons perform the same physical action but with different intensity of *moha*. The karmic debt increases with the increase in the intensity of *moha*. Now we take an example in which a person plays different physical roles in the performance of an action. Consider three cases of involvement of a person in the same action: he performs the action himself; he causes someone else to perform the action, or he only gives his consent to someone else performing it. How does the karmic debt vary with the degree of involvement in performing the action?"

"He'll increase the karmic debt not only when he himself performs the action, but also when he provokes the action, and when he only gives his consent for the action. The more direct is his involvement in the action, the larger is the karmic debt."

"Think about this illustration. Two persons carry out the same physical action of donating identical amounts of money to a charity, but one does so with more fervor than the other. Are they going to have the same karmic debt?"

"I suppose the person who donates with less fervor should accumulate less karmic debt, but I'm confused. Donation to any charity is an act of altruism. How can altruistic actions be the cause of karmic debt?"

"All actions, including altruistic actions, involve *moha*, hence cause karmic debt. As altruistic actions with less fervor are performed with mild *moha*, they add little to karmic debt."

"If altruistic actions also create karmic debt, then how can one liquidate karmic debt?"

"You are not alone in being confused, Jason. Most people fail to comprehend this subtlety of the karma doctrine. If good actions also create karmic debt, then how can one liquidate it?"

"Aren't you saying that no living being can get rid of its karmic debt?"

"I am not saying that. There are currently infinite pure souls in the universe, and infinite worldly souls will become pure souls by annihilating their karmic debt in the future. The process of liquidation of karmic debt can be explained by describing the interaction between the newly attached and previously attached karmas. Since this is an important concept to study in more detail, we will save it for tomorrow. Meanwhile, tell me, why do you think that altruistic actions are good actions?"

"I consider those actions that cause desirable consequences as good actions. Altruistic actions are good actions as they have desirable consequence of going to Heaven after death. But I am unable to reconcile between the concepts of the desirable consequence of going to Heaven and the increase in karmic debt by performing good actions."

"Jason, your answer to the question why altruistic actions

are good actions is brilliant! I feel proud to guide you in discovering the karma doctrine. It is logical to think that one should not go to heaven with larger karmic debt. You will learn, probably the day after tomorrow, that the karma doctrine also reveals that human beings can transmigrate to heaven in their next life by performing altruistic actions in the present life. One final question before we conclude today's discourse. What are the material and efficient causes of the new modes of your soul and body?"

"The new or post-modes of my soul and body depend on the old or pre-modes of soul and body. The pre-modes of my soul and body are the material causes of the post-modes of my soul and body. The three psychical karmas and the four physiological karmas, as well as environmental factors, are the efficient causes of the post-modes of my soul and body."

"Well done, Jason. That concludes today's session."

I leave Guru's dwelling feeling rather agitated. What factors influence my own karma, I wonder. I can be a rather passionate person in both good and bad ways. For instance, I love learning new things, but I'm sometimes impatient about reaching goals. Am I working against myself with these passions? Is there anything I can do to influence my karma positively? Guru, you're leaving me walking on a tightrope of thought today, do you realize that? I'll be eager to hear more about whether I can influence my own karma and, if so, how. If not, what are the implications — am I just a puppet of invisible karma?

Notes

1. In Jainism there are two separate karmas for obscuring perception and obscuring knowledge. They have been combined into one "knowledge-obscuring" karma here to simplify the discussion.

Chapter 9

Karmic Field

I've been contemplating the karma doctrine since yesterday, and I think the doctrine now makes sense to me. I can understand how karma serves as a carrier and deliverer of the universal consequences of actions, but many questions keep coming to my mind. I've been pondering them, even during my sleep. One of them is about universal consequences. Can universal consequences of past actions, and hence past karmic debt, be altered by new actions?

After I arrive at Guru's dwelling, Guru asks me whether I have any questions. I immediately ask, "Are universal consequences of past actions unchangeable or can they be altered by future actions?"

"The nature of your question suggests that you are acquiring a good understanding of the metaphysical model of the karma doctrine, but it is still incomplete. We will work towards completing your understanding today. Before I answer your question about changeability of universal consequences of past actions by future actions, let me first hear your ideas."

"Okay. In our legal system, the sentences of prisoners are sometimes reduced due to their good conduct in prison. Likewise, it seems reasonable to assume that present actions should influence the consequences of past actions," I reply.

"That is a reasonable extrapolation. However, the prisoners' sentences are ruled by man-made laws that are non-universal, while universal consequences are governed by the universal karma doctrine."

"True. Let me try to explain my thinking through another illustration."

"Go ahead, Jason."

"Suppose I commit a very heinous action for which the time of fruition of the karma is so long that it'll take several rebirths for its fruition. After committing the crime, I regret my atrocious behavior, repent, and become a completely different person, almost saintly. Although I've become saintly, I'll still have several reincarnations for fruition of old karma related to the heinous action unless my present actions can alter the universal consequences of my past actions. Surely the saintly behavior has some impact on that."

"Your logic is correct, Jason. Present actions do influence the universal consequences of past actions. Let us look at your illustration a little more closely. It implies that heinous action is a bad action and saintly actions are good actions. The problem of distinguishing good and evil actions is an age-old problem. Since the karma doctrine deals with actions and consequences, an assessment of the success of the doctrine in resolving the issue of good and evil actions will go a long way in evaluating the significance of the doctrine itself. Because the karma doctrine is an explanatory hypothesis to resolve the problem of actions and their consequences and is not empirically verifiable, there would seem to be little reason to advocate the doctrine should it fail to answer the problem of defining good and evil actions. What do you think, Jason?"

"If even altruistic actions create karmic debt, as you pointed out yesterday, it doesn't seem possible to come up with a definition of good actions based on karmic debt."

"I understand your concern. Although both good and evil actions lead to karmic debt, there are major differences between the effects of the newly attached karma of good versus evil actions, according to the following process. The old, attached karma undergoes various processes of transformation due to the newly attached karma, including the modification of the intensity of *moha*, and hence karmic debt, of the old attached karma. The application of this understanding—that the karma of actions newly attached to the karmic body either increases or decreases the intensity of *moha*, and hence karmic debt, of the old karma—leads to a consistent explanation of good and evil actions, involving the effect of interaction between new and old karma on the karmic debt. The explanation of this interaction between new and old karma requires invocation of two more extrinsic properties of the karmic body, so you will have to be very attentive to this discourse."

"Uh-oh! I thought we were done with the extrinsic properties of the karmic body. How many more extrinsic properties are there?"

"Relax, Jason. Though there are many more extrinsic properties of the karmic body, we need only two more for the development of the karmic model. The attached karma of past actions creates a karmic 'field' inside and around the karmic body, like an electric field around electrically charged particles. In the same way that the electric field produced by charged particles is affected by introducing additional charged particles, the karmic field created by formerly attached karma is influenced by the new karma of subsequent actions. This process continuously and automatically 'updates' the karmic field and alters the intensity of *moha*, and hence karmic debt, of the old karma. Therefore, the intensity of *moha* and karmic debt of karma at the time of its attachment to the karmic body need not be identical to the intensity of *moha* and karmic debt of karma when it finally comes to fruition and detaches from the karmic body. In other words, the directives of the universal consequences of an action stored in karma at the time of its attachment to the karmic body can be different than the eventual karmic consequences delivered at the time of its fruition."

I nod while wondering at the intricacy of the karma doctrine. He continues, "The interaction between the karmic fields of the old and new karma is one of the most important presuppositions of the karma doctrine. The liquidation of karmic debt is not possible without this interaction, which we must understand to complete the unfinished model of the karma doctrine. For that we need to know the two additional extrinsic properties of the karmic body: 'increased realization' and 'decreased realization.' The property of 'increased realization' deals with the process that increases the time and intensity of delivery of consequences of the old karma. Similarly, the property of 'decreased realization' deals with the process that decreases the time and intensity of delivery of consequences of the old karma. The new karma of the new action has the capability to affect the intensity of *moha*, and hence the time and intensity of delivery of consequences, of the old karma of the old actions, through these two extrinsic properties of increased and decreased realization. The process of interaction between the new and old karma, including the modification in the intensity of *moha* of the old karma, should provide the basis for defining good and evil actions. A new action whose newly attached karma decreases the average intensity of *moha*, and hence the karmic debt, of the old, attached karma through the property of decreased realization is termed a good action. Based on this definition of a good action, can you provide a similar definition of an evil action?"

"I think so. A new action whose newly attached karma increases the average intensity of *moha*, and hence the karmic debt, of the old, attached karma through the property of increased realization is termed an evil action."

"Excellent, Jason. Let us now analyze how we can use these definitions of good and evil actions to manage our karmic debt. Newly attached karma decreases the average intensity of *moha* of the formerly attached karma if the intensity of *moha* of the new action is less than the average intensity of *moha* of the old karma. Such a new action is a good action as it decreases the average intensity of *moha*, and hence the karmic debt, of the old, attached karma. The milder the intensity of *moha* of the new action, the larger would be the decrease in the karmic debt of the old karma. Similarly, the newly attached karma increases the average intensity of *moha* of the formerly attached karma if the intensity of *moha* of the new action is more than the average intensity of *moha* of the old karma. Such a new action is an evil action, as it increases the average intensity of *moha*, and hence the karmic debt, of the old, attached karma. The larger the intensity of *moha* of the new action, the larger the increase in the karmic debt of the old karma. Subhuman beings decrease their karmic debt through the property of decreased realization, as will be explained in a later discussion. Does this make sense to you, Jason?"

"I think so. If goodness or evilness of an action depends on the intensity of *moha*, and hence karmic debt, of the old karma, an altruistic action can be a good action for a person who carries a large karmic debt and an evil action for a person who carries a small karmic debt. Is that right?"

"Yes. Whether an altruistic action is good or evil depends on the karmic debt the doer carries. This finding has an important implication on one's spiritual development. For permanent spiritual advancement, the intensity of *moha* of each successive action should be less than the intensity of *moha* of the previous action."

"I believe I now understand how I can influence my karma positively and the technique of decreasing karmic debt and hence, enhancing inner peace. One should perform successive actions with diminishing intensity of *moha*."

"I am glad that you have understood the interaction between the new and old karma and its relevance to inner peace. Let us now analyze the effect of good actions on the rate of fruition of karmic particles. Suppose during the next few days a person on average performs more good actions than evil actions, so that the intensity of *moha* of his old karma decreases. What is the effect of the decrease of the intensity of *moha* on the average time of fruition of karma?"

"I suppose the average time of fruition of karma decreases with the decrease in the intensity of *moha*."

"What is the effect of the decrease in the time of fruition on the rate of fruition of the karmic particles?"

"There would be only one way for the same number of karmic particles to come to fruition in the shorter period due to the decrease in the average time of fruition; that is, a higher number of karmic particles should come to fruition in the shorter period. In other words, the average rate of number of karmic particles that detach from the karmic body increases with more good actions than evil actions."

"You are right. Now tell me the effect of the decrease in the intensity of *moha* on the intensity of delivery of consequences of karma."

"It follows that the intensity of delivery of consequences of karma would decrease with the decrease in the intensity of *moha* of karma."

"Bravo, Jason. What is the effect of the decrease in the intensity of delivery of consequences of karma on the intensity of *moha* of the new action and hence the new karma?"

"The intensity of *moha* of the new action would be controlled by the intensity of delivery of the nature-deluding karma. A decrease in the latter would cause the new action to have a decreased intensity of *moha*, which in turn promotes good action."

"Excellent! You can see that the performance of more good actions than evil actions, on average, has three effects: One, it decreases the intensity of *moha*, and hence karmic debt, of the old karma. Two, it decreases the time of fruition of karma, which results in an increase in the average number of karmic particles that detach from the karmic body, which in turn causes an increase in the rate of reduction of karmic debt. Three, it causes a decrease in the intensity of *moha* of the new action, which in turn attaches new karma with a lower intensity of *moha*, and hence accrues less karmic debt. Can you describe similar effects of the performance of more evil actions than good actions, on average?"

"I'll try. The performance of more evil actions than good actions, on average, would have three effects: One, it increases the intensity of *moha*, and hence karmic debt, of the old karma. Two, it increases the time of fruition of karma, which results in a decrease in the average number of karmic particles that detach from the karmic body, which in turn causes a decrease in the rate of reduction of karmic debt. Three, it causes an increase in the intensity of *moha* of the new action, which in turn attaches new karma with a higher intensity of *moha*, and hence accrues more karmic debt."

"We now have all different components of the karmic model governed by universal laws, which provide an innate moral order to living beings. Based on the presuppositions described in earlier discourses, the metaphysical model of the karma doctrine can be summarized as follows:

All space in the universe, including the space within body cells, is packed with karmic matter. The amount of karmic matter attracted by the karmic body at any instant due to *yoga*—the physical action of mind, vocal organ and body—depends on the intensity of the volitional activities with which the physical action is performed. Nonliving karmic matter upon association with the soul transforms into living karmic matter, called karma. Karma transmutes into seven main types that carry different universal consequences of actions. The three psychical karmas affect the properties of knowledge, spiritual power, inner peace, and *moha* of soul. Two psychical karmas, knowledge-obscuring and spiritual-power-obscuring karmas, respectively, prevent the full manifestation of the properties of knowledge and spiritual power by obscuring them, as clouds obscure the sunlight. The third psychical karma, nature-deluding karma, prevents the full manifestation of the property of inner peace of soul by defiling it with *moha*.

The four physiological karmas—feeling-determining, power-determining, lifespan-determining, and physique-determining karmas—affect the four physiological properties of senses, power, lifespan, and physique of living matter of the body, respectively.

Due to *moha*, the various types of karma remain attached to the karmic body for different durations. The duration of karmic bondage with the karmic body and the intensity of delivery of consequences of karma increase with the increase in the intensity of *moha* with which the action is performed. At the end of the duration of attachment, karma executes the karmic consequences, detaches from the karmic body, and transforms back into nonliving karmic matter. The delivery of consequences of karma results in new actions which in turn bind the new karma to the karmic body and the cycle continues.

Karma undergoes various processes that are realized by the extrinsic properties of the karmic body. The various processes undertaken by karma develop an interactive karmic field within the karmic body. Although the new karma of the new action attached to the karmic body comes to fruition in the future, the extrinsic properties of the karmic body instantly and automatically 'update' the karmic field so that this effect of new karma happens instantaneously. The newly attached karma of good new actions decreases the intensity of *moha*, and hence decreases the duration of bondage and decreases the intensity of consequences of old attached karma. This process of modification of karma decreases the karmic debt of the old karma, increases the rate of reduction of karmic debt due to an increase in the average number of karmic particles that detach from the karmic body, and attaches the new karma with a lower intensity of *moha*. In contrast, the newly attached karma of new evil actions increases the intensity of *moha*, and hence increases the duration of bondage and increases the intensity of consequences of old attached karma. This process of modification of karma increases the karmic debt of the old karma, decreases the rate of reduction of karmic debt due to a decrease in the average number of karmic particles that detach from the karmic body, and attaches the new karma with a higher intensity of *moha*. Lastly, karmic debt is affected not only when one performs the action, but also when one provokes the action, when one indirectly participates in or prepares for the action, and when one only gives consent for the action. Human beings have the ability and power to manage their karmic debt by managing their actions that include physical actions, i.e., *yoga*, and intentions and emotions, i.e., *moha*."

Guru pauses for a moment as I raise my finger, but he continues, "I know what you are going to say. You want me to end today's discourse as you need time to absorb everything. You pointed out your wish at the right moment, as I was done with the summary of the karma doctrine. Contemplation and reflection on the complexity of the karma doctrine will help you to understand its intricacy. Because we will talk tomorrow about false belief of self, you should read about ego on the Internet."

I sigh and quickly exit from the Guru's room. I have so much to ponder and study about ego, while my head is still spinning. Coincidentally, I don't need to go to the library to study ego, as I am reading a book that deals with various aspects of ego. I head to the park to study the book and prepare my notes.

While going to the park, I contemplate on the intensity of *moha* during my passion of producing watercolor paintings. It is an enjoyable hobby for me, and it is a very meditative activity that promotes a sense of equanimity with possibly mild *moha*. I do notice, though, with some inner amusement, that when I produce a painting that I feel fails in some way, I get quite disappointed — which I assume means that I'm experiencing high-intensity *moha*. However, when a painting succeeds in some way, I get quite excited to share it with someone and full of joy — which I assume also have high-intensity of *moha*. I suspect that if I didn't experience much emotion either way, I might not paint at all. However, I now understand that I need to cultivate a joy during painting with *moha* that becomes milder and milder with time.

Chapter 10

Mastering Karma

I've learned a great deal about the karma doctrine in the last eight discussions, including a completely different understanding of the "good" and "evil" actions. I now know that I'm here in the lifeform of a human being due to my actions in my previous lives. Is my life going to be better than the lives of most people who have no knowledge of the karma doctrine? I know that knowledge of the karma doctrine alone isn't going to lead me to achieve inner peace unless I apply it in my daily life. But I don't know how to use this knowledge in my daily activities. I reach the Guru's dwelling with this dilemma in my mind.

As I take my seat, Guru asks me, "Do you now have faith in rebirth?"

"I think I have a better understanding of the karma doctrine, but I'm not sure about the rebirth process. I need to implement the teachings of the doctrine in my daily life, but I don't know how."

"I understand your dilemma. Many people believe that they understand the karma doctrine, but they do not have unconditional faith in reincarnation. For the karma doctrine to be meaningful, the presupposition of rebirth is indispensable. Do you ever think about your lifeform in the next life?"

"Never."

"What we believe usually dictates our actions and attitudes, which in turn generate our emotional responses. We are very attached to our beliefs. Our belief that our body, not our soul, is more important to our wellbeing stems from the fact that we have been exploring only the physical reality with our senses, not the nonphysical realities with our soul. Most of our actions are limited to caring for our body. We wear clothes that are soft to our skin, eat foods that are tasty to our tongue, smell odors that are pleasant to our nose, surround ourselves with things that look beautiful to our eyes, and listen to sound that is pleasing to our ears. There is no doubt that we must take care of our body, but we also have a soul. If people could be happy by satisfying only their five senses, then many people in the world would be happy, but that is not the case. Even people who have countless resources to please their senses suffer from mental tension, emotional anxiety, and depression. Do you know why you never thought about your lifeform in the next life?"

"Because I had no knowledge of the karma doctrine, and I didn't believe in reincarnation."

"Jason, your answer implies that people who know the karma doctrine and believe in reincarnation must sometimes think about their lifeform in the next life. But this conclusion is incorrect. There are millions of Hindus, Buddhists, and Jains who know about the karma doctrine and believe in reincarnation but never think of their lifeform in the next life. I myself only recently started thinking about my lifeform in the next life. Now that you have some knowledge of the karma doctrine, can you figure out why?"

"Does it have something to do with the fruition of my nature-deluding karma?"

"Yes! Upon fruition of the belief-deluding karma, a subtype of the nature-deluding karma, human beings have a false belief of self, i.e., ego. This is due to disruption of their innate ability to perceive truth, and they never think of their lifeform in the next life. Only a few people, who are not slaves to their egos, think about their lifeform in the next life.

"Each of us has an account in the universal karmic bank. Our net karmic debt in the karmic bank at any time depends on our actions. Each time we perform a good action, our karmic debt decreases, while an evil action increases it. We are normally born into this worldly life with a larger karmic debt than the threshold required to be aware of our soul. If we carry out more evil than good actions, our karmic debt grows and remains above that threshold. Consequently, we keep performing actions to please our senses and ignoring our souls and, thus, remain spiritually unawakened slaves of ego. On the other hand, if we carry out more good than evil actions, our karmic debt decreases and eventually falls below the threshold, allowing us to begin to perceive the truth. Consequently, we keep performing actions that bring about spiritual growth and, thus, become spiritually awakened masters of karma. Now, tell me what you have learned about ego on the Internet."

I turn on my laptop, open the file on ego, and read. "Ego is the false belief of self. When one's mind has bound the concept of self with a thing, the mind is in the state of ego. That thing can be an entity, or it can be a concept or thought. We tend to call our self by the name 'I' and don't discriminate between what we call me and what we call mine. In childhood our mind binds the concept of self with 'my' blanket or toy, and later in adulthood with 'my' wife, 'my' son, 'my' house, and so on. In addition to relatives and material objects, we identify self with 'my' body.

"Ego expresses itself in various ways. Due to ego, we develop consuming desires for things concerned with our bodies and remain engrossed in attachment to worldly objects and gratification of our senses. Unfulfilled desires lead to anger, jealousy, depression, anxiety, dissatisfaction, and resentment."

I pause for a moment and ask, "Should I go on to present the awakening process?"

"I am curious, Jason. Did you find this information on the Internet or have you been reading something else that deals with ego and spiritual awakening?"

I'm amazed by the Guru's astuteness. How did he know where I got my information? Also, I had the misimpression that Guru's knowledge was limited to the karma doctrine. Apparently, he's also familiar with the Western concept of spiritual awakening.

"You're right that I've been doing some other reading on my own."

"I am impressed to learn of your interest in spiritual awakening. Go ahead with what you read about the awakening process."

I begin reading from my laptop. "Ego arises when belief of Beingness, which is formless consciousness, gets attached to form, e.g., body. Since ego is a false belief of self, ego does not have spiritual awareness. Moreover, ego depends upon thought, and spiritual awareness is experienced, not thought.

"According to my source the initiation of the awakening process is an act of grace. It says you can't make it happen nor can you prepare yourself for it. You don't have to become worthy first. There's nothing you can do about awakening."

"Jason, I thought you were not inclined to believe in God, which would make this explanation, based on God's grace, untenable. What if you considered the awakening process through the lens of the karma doctrine?"

"Guru, you're right that I prefer a logical explanation, instead of invoking God's grace. But I need your help to explain the awakening process by the karma doctrine."

"It is actually quite logical. The intensity of ego fluctuates with time. There are times when it is strong and times when it is weak. It is possible to initiate the awakening process when ego is weak. Do you remember the karma that controls the intensity of ego?"

"I do. It's the belief-deluding karma, a subtype of the nature-deluding karma."

"Very good, Jason. The soul's apprehension of truth is hindered by fruition of belief-deluding karma. Keep in mind that the intensity of all karmas at fruition, including the belief-deluding karma, fluctuates with time between mild and strong. If the intensity of the belief-deluding karma is strong at fruition, the ego is strong, and human beings are unable to initiate spiritual awakening. Fortunately, there are periods, though of small duration, in most humans' lives when the intensity of belief-deluding karma is mild at fruition. Since the intensity of manifestation of *moha* decreases during these periods, the grip of ego on the human mind weakens, and the possibility of initiating the awakening process increases. However, this state itself, though necessary, is not enough to initiate the awakening process. One also needs strong willpower, which is controlled by spiritual power, to initiate the awakening process. Which karma controls spiritual power?"

"It's the spiritual-power-obscuring karma."

"Yes. Attainment of strong spiritual power, which occurs when the intensity of spiritual-power-obscuring karma is mild at fruition, is needed to initiate the awakening process. Fortunately, there are some periods, of small duration, in most humans' lives when the intensity of both belief-deluding and spiritual-power-obscuring karmas are mild at fruition. During these periods, the intensity of manifestation of both inner peace and spiritual power is sufficiently strong to overcome ego and initiate awakening by suppressing nature-deluding karma.

"Though both inner peace and spiritual power are strong, without any proper circumstances that serve as an efficient cause to activate awakening, one is likely to miss it. Teachings about the true nature of the soul from a spiritual teacher or experiences, such as the loss of a beloved friend, or the sight of extreme suffering, or remembrance of a past life, can serve as suitable efficient causes. When all three attainments — strong inner peace, strong spiritual power, and circumstances — are realized by the soul, for a brief period, the belief-deluding karma is suppressed without fruition. As a result, ego is temporarily purged, and the soul experiences the glorious vision of reality that is a brief transient awakening."

"Wow! How long will I have to wait to experience one of

these brief transient spiritual awakenings?"

"We all experience brief flashes of strange clarity with varying frequency when the intensity of consequences of both the belief-deluding and spiritual-power-obscuring karmas is mild. For example, maybe you are hiking in Yellowstone and all of a sudden it feels as if you and the trees, birds, and living beings all around you have identical souls with varying karmic debt. But we ignore these flashes and do not talk about them, as we are busy in the constant hustle-bustle of our daily life; plus, nobody told us how to interpret these flashes. These flashes are indications of our potential for spiritual growth, provided we find time in our daily routine to recognize them. The quicker you learn to master your karma, the sooner you begin to experience brief transient spiritual awakenings."

"What is the key to mastering karma?"

"The key to mastering karma is to perform actions that reduce karmic debt, which is determined by the intensity of *moha* associated with actions. Do you remember the constituents of the soul's property of *moha*?"

"I do. They are ego, negative passions and quasi-passions but I still don't understand the distinction between passions and quasi-passions."

"The quasi-passions remain present until every trace of the major passions like anger or greed is rooted out. The degree to which the quasi-passions are manifested decreases with spiritual advancement; hence a spiritually advanced monk is likely to feel sorrow or fear or pleasure much less than ordinary people."

"Thanks, it makes sense."

"Very good, Jason. Nature-deluding karma defiles the soul's property of inner peace with *moha*. In addition to controlling ego by distorting one's belief of what really matters, nature-deluding karma controls negative passions and quasi-passions manifested in temperament. Temperament includes equanimity, which is an element of inner peace. Only nonviolent actions, including actions of the mind, reduce karmic debt. We need to get rid of the false belief, caused by ego, that our body, rather than our soul, is most pertinent to inner peace, in order to pursue the lifestyle of a nonviolent person."

"Can I live a nonviolent life while studying at Stanford and pursuing a career afterwards?"

"Your question implies that you are not sure which actions qualify for nonviolent actions. Let me hear your understanding of nonviolence."

"To me, nonviolence is not killing another human being."

"Like most people, your perception of nonviolence is very rudimentary. Most of us do not kill human beings, but this does not mean that we are nonviolent. On the contrary, most of us are violent. We directly, or indirectly through others, hurt, harm, injure or kill. We not only do this to human beings, but other living beings also. We hurt others not by bodily injury alone, but many other ways, including verbal and mental abuse. We hurt others physically by beating, mutilating, wounding, and killing; verbally by speaking harsh and unpleasant words; and mentally by oppressing and harboring ill feelings. We cause suffering to others by acquiring more than our fair share of limited natural resources. We harm others by lying, bearing false witness, using abrasive language, stealing their possessions, selling poorly made goods, and so on. The practice of nonviolence requires refraining from all such violent actions, including desires and motives connected with such actions. According to Jain scriptures, our actions should be governed by five types of abstinence: abstention from (1) harming or killing living beings, (2) false or hurtful speech, (3) theft and illegal or immoral transactions, (4) unchaste sexual acts, and (5) craving and hoarding worldly possessions."

"You are telling me what I shouldn't do, but I want to know what I should do."

"Renouncing violent actions obviously requires accepting nonviolent actions. Negating desires and motives to harm life implies reverence for life, which in turn develops compassion and equanimity towards life. Nonviolence inculcates feelings of benevolence and harmony. You should perform thoughtful actions that include kindness but detachment."

"So, I grew up with parents who told me to give with a joyful heart. But is a joyful heart detached enough?"

"As there are degrees of attachment, so there are degrees of detachment. Only an action performed with no *moha* qualifies as with complete detachment."

"Okay, I have a hypothetical question. Suppose I get a high salaried job after my graduation from Stanford. Can I lead a nonviolent life while running after money in my profession?"

"Jason, the answer to your question is hidden in your question. I am surprised that you did not find it. Who would run after money— a person operating out of ego or without ego?"

"The answer is obvious. People operating out of ego are never satisfied. They always need more money."

"We run after money because we operate out of ego, a false belief of self. If we carry the misbelief that the body, rather than the soul, is most pertinent to long-term happiness, we keep on maximizing wealth to experience momentary episodes of physical happiness. Limitless desire for wealth is a major obstacle to achieving spiritual growth and causes much tension in life. The earlier we realize that the soul, not the body, is relevant to inner peace and control of ego, the sooner we stop running after wealth and begin performing nonviolent actions that promote spiritual growth and increase the duration of inner peace. As a result of this true perception, our attitude toward life and outlook toward worldly objects turns out to be completely different."

Guru continues, "We have to choose between two intentions:

one, the maximization of wealth to experience episodes of physical happiness, and the other, maximization of the duration of inner peace. The goal of maximization of wealth is achieved by violent actions that increase the karmic debt and decrease the duration of inner peace. The karmic debt of a person who performs on average more violent than nonviolent actions increases with time. Consequently, the duration of inner peace decreases with time. Such a person becomes increasingly less happy in life. On the contrary, the goal of maximization of duration of inner peace is achieved by nonviolent actions. The karmic debt of a person who performs on average more nonviolent than violent actions decreases with time. Consequently, the duration of inner peace increases with time. Such a person experiences a more long-term spiritual happiness."

"Wow! Mastering karma is not as easy as I thought. I'll need some additional time to absorb it."

"This is a good time to end today's discourse. I am glad to hear that you plan to spend some time reflecting on the karmic process. Tomorrow we will continue our discussion on mastering karma. And if time permits, we will talk about possible lifeforms in the next life."

I bow my head to Guru and leave for the campsite. I don't need to go to the library as he gave me no reading assignment today, but I have plenty to think about.

Chapter 11

Lifeforms

I never thought that I would be so fascinated by the karma doctrine that I'd be thinking about it all the time. I'm trying to get some sleep but somehow can't stop pondering the awakening process. It makes sense to me that a person is spiritually awakened, i.e., without ego, when belief-deluding karma is either suppressed or annihilated. I understand about a person experiencing a brief transient spiritual awakening during the suppression of belief-deluding karma. Then the grip of ego on the mind rebuilds and takes control over the person's behavior. And, if belief-deluding karma is eliminated from the karmic body, the person enjoys permanent spiritual awakening. These ideas excite me. Finally, I fall asleep, while still pondering the suppression process of karmas.

Morning comes, and I reach the Guru's abode with many questions on my mind. As soon as I sit at my designated seat, I ask Guru, "Can one suppress other karmas besides belief-deluding karma?"

"I am glad that you asked this question, as I was actually going to ask you that same question. Tell me what you think."

"I think, why not? Other karmas should also be suppressed at times."

"Can you imagine the consequences of suppression of the physiological karmas that determine the new modes of living matter? During the period of their suppression, there could be no change in the modes of the living matter, because the entire system of one's body would stop functioning. One would not be able to do any physical activities, including respiration, metabolization and digestion. In fact, no karmas, other than nature-deluding karma, can be suppressed."

"Does this mean that not only can't one suppress other karmas, but also can't eliminate them?"

"Only the lifespan-determining karma of the present lifeform is eliminated. The elimination of the lifespan-determining karma of the present lifeform results in sudden death. At the same moment, the lifespan-determining karma for the lifeform in the next life binds the karmic body."

"So, how does one attain liberation from the cycle of birth and death without eliminating karmas?"

"What I have been explaining is the suppression and elimination processes of karmas of living beings who are still revolving in the rebirth process. However, one must eliminate all karmas, i.e., annihilate all karmic debt, to achieve liberation. One first eliminates all psychical karmas, including nature-deluding karma. *Moha* is eliminated along with nature-deluding karma. New karma, and hence new karmic debt, stop attaching to the karmic body once *moha* is eliminated. One only performs actions without *moha*, i.e., *yoga*. Eventually, one eliminates all physiological karmas and attains liberation."

"Can any living being attain liberation?"

"Only humans have the unique inherent capability of transforming their behavior and managing their karmic debt, and hence achieve liberation. According to the karma doctrine, the purpose of human life is the minimization and eventual annihilation of the individual's karmic debt."

"Since we're supposed to choose between good and evil actions, does the karma doctrine deal with ethics?"

"Ethics is an integral part of the karma doctrine. We need to implement the principles of ethics in our daily conduct for spiritual development and karmic debt reduction. Remember we talked yesterday about nonviolent actions with the five types of abstinence? They are based on the principles of ethics, as presented in Jain scriptures. These principles of ethics are based on the presupposition that living beings will continue wandering in the cycle of life, death, and rebirth as long as they carry their karmic debt with their soul. Jason, based on these principles, what kind of conduct is righteous conduct?"

"Since the karmic debt depends on the intensity of *yoga*-plus-*moha*, it seems that conduct that diminishes the intensity of *yoga* and *moha* should be considered power."

"Very good, Jason. Righteous conduct is required for the process of self-purification, and it consists of an external aspect that is related to *yoga* and an internal aspect that is associated with *moha*. As *yoga* is related to the physiological property of power, which is always assisted by the physiological property of sense, external conduct is managed by sense restraint and Physical. Internal conduct is controlled by managing *moha*, which in turn requires repeated practice of self-disciplinary methods."

"What do you mean by sense restraint?"

"Sense restraint means control over the sense organs to decrease attachment to our body. It has been elegantly said that the canals of the senses, overflowing with the water of desire, nurture the poisonous tree of desires which heavily deludes the soul. It is up to us how we use our senses. We can use them to either increase or decrease our *moha*. The purpose of the sense organs is the survival of the body, but we misuse our senses, as can be shown by a cursory scrutiny of our conduct in daily life."

"How do we misuse our senses?"

"Consider the sense of touch, for example. The tactile-sensory system feels temperature, roughness, and hardness. We have these sensations so that we can avoid hot, cold, rough, and hard substances that can injure our body. If we cannot sense heat, we are likely to burn our hand by touching a hot skillet. If we cannot sense cold, we are likely to have frostbite from exposing our body to freezing temperatures. If we cannot feel hardness and roughness, we are likely to injure our body on hard and rough surfaces. The use of the tactile-sensory system to protect our body from getting injured is one thing, but its use to please and comfort our body is an entirely different matter. The use of simple clothes to protect our body is understandable, but the use of expensive designer clothes shows our attachment to our body due to ego, which increases our *moha*. The same logic can be used for items such as ornaments, jewelry, and cosmetics that we use to beautify our body. Simple living and noble thinking should be our motto for living."

"Are you saying that no pleasant sensations are allowed whatsoever?"

"You are not a pure soul as long you have association with the body. The complete liquidation of karmic debt occurs at no *moha*, i.e., no pleasant sensations whatsoever."

"Do we misuse other senses also?"

"Yes, we do. The intensity of our *moha* depends on our control over our senses. I will give a few more examples. If we have no control over our taste buds, we develop cravings for food, which in turn increases our *moha* towards food. If we do not have control over our olfactory sense, we develop attachment to certain smells, which in turn increases our *moha* for things like cosmetics and similar products. We need to have control over the vision-sensory system. Otherwise we misuse it for things like reading unworthy books and watching demeaning entertainment programs. With our hearing sense we might use it to hear spiritual sermons that help to diminish our *moha* or debasing music that increases our *moha*. We should have control over our five senses so that we do not use them in activities that increase our *moha*."

"Okay. That makes sense. Now tell me about power restraint."

"Power restraint requires control over physical actions of the body, vocal organs, and mind. As we use our sense restraints to control our *moha*, similarly we should use our power restraints to control our *moha* by performing actions following the five types of abstinence discussed yesterday."

"Now I understand how to control external conduct by sense and power restraints. Tell me how to control internal conduct to manage *moha*."

"The powerful forces of sensual attractions, desires, and delusions constantly drag the soul toward objects of sensual pleasure and lead to attachment towards worldly objects. Hence, one should concentrate primarily on reducing and eventually destroying *moha*, as it is the root cause of all evils. This, in turn, requires repeated practices of self-disciplinary methods, such as of renunciation, expiation, and attainment of equanimity. Since it is difficult to change one's way of life, exercise in self-discipline needs to be constantly practiced with perseverance."

"Whew! That sounds like hard but worthwhile work. I must comprehend the terms you just described to practice the self-disciplinary methods. Can you explain what you mean by renunciation?"

"Each soul prior to becoming a pure soul is a worldly soul because of egoistic feelings of 'my' and 'mine,' the false belief of self, and attachment to body and possessions. To practice the method of renunciation, one resolves to renounce all egoistic thoughts, feeling of attachment to body and possessions, and unwholesome, sinful, and unrighteous conduct. One contemplates that the intrinsic nature of one's worldly soul is the same as that of the pure soul."

"What can you tell me about the method of expiation?"

"We all are liable to make mistakes, and we have to be aware of our mistakes to amend them. One must review, at the end of the day, one's daily activities and see where one has slipped. One resolves not to repeat them. Expiation means atonement for one's sins and unwholesome inclinations, and purification of one's soul. Since negative passions are the real enemies of the soul and the main cause of karmic debt, expiation consists of conquering negative passions: anger by forgiveness, pride by humility, deceit by straightforwardness, and greed by contentment."

"I think I understand the term equanimity. The purpose of equanimity is the cultivation of equal goodwill and sympathy towards all religions, races and castes, and genders. Am I right?"

"You are partly correct, Jason. The purpose of equanimity also is to regard all living beings as equal with one's own self and to maintain evenness of mind on all occasions, favorable and adverse. The means of developing equanimity are restraints and abstinence and meditation. We have discussed restraints and abstinence earlier. Meditation is the concentration of restless mind on the intrinsic nature and real attributes of the self."

"My next question is: Which karmic factor determines one's lifeform in the next life?"

"The karmic debt at death determines the lifeform in the next life. A living being with less karmic debt at death will have a more advanced lifeform in the next life."

"What do you mean by a more advanced lifeform?"

"An advanced lifeform means a physically and spiritually developed living being. The physical development of a living being is characterized by the number of its senses and its mind; only five-sensed beings have mind. A living being with a greater number of senses has a more physically developed body. The spiritual development of a living being is characterized by the average intensity of its *moha*, hence the karmic debt. The milder the average intensity of *moha*, hence the karmic debt, the greater the spiritual growth. A more advanced lifeform means a living being with a greater number of senses, a mind, and greater spiritual growth."

"How many lifeforms are there in the universe?"

"Living beings are classified into two types: fine and gross. The fine living beings are only one-sensed. We call them sub-microorganisms. They permeate all space in the universe and are imperceptible to the human senses. Gross living beings range from one-sensed to five-sensed subhuman beings, plus five-sensed human, infernal, and celestial beings. There are, therefore, nine types of living beings: one type of fine living being and eight types of gross living beings. Living beings have senses ranging from one to five; five-sensed living beings have a mind also."

Guru hands me a piece of paper which includes a table of living beings. He goes on to explain the table.

Examples of Different Categories of Living Beings

Types of Living Beings	Example
1. Sub-microorganism	Bacteria
2. One-sensed subhuman being	Plants
3. Two-sensed subhuman being	Earthworms, Shells
4. Three-sensed subhuman being	Ants
5. Four-sensed subhuman being	Reptiles, Flies, Bees
6. Five-sensed infernal being	
7. Five-sensed subhuman being	Animals, Birds, Fishes
8. Five-sensed human being	
9. Five-sensed celestial being	

"One-sensed sub-microorganisms have the least advanced lifeform and the maximum karmic debt. Five-sensed living beings have a highly developed lifeform and carry a lesser amount of karmic debt. As all four types of five-sensed living beings have the same number of five senses and a mind, the ranking of their lifeform cannot be determined by the number of senses. The ranking of their lifeform is determined by the karmic debt they carry to the next life. Two of the five-sensed lifeforms belong to less-developed lifeform and the other two to more-developed lifeform. Can you identify more-developed lifeforms that require less karmic debt to reincarnate in those lifeforms?"

"According to my understanding, human and celestial

lifeforms are more advanced than subhuman and infernal lifeforms. A living being with less karmic debt transmigrates to either human or celestial lifeform, and a living being with more karmic debt transmigrates to either subhuman or infernal lifeform."

"Bravo, Jason. You can see that as per karma doctrine, a human being transmigrates to celestial lifeform by performing good actions that reduce karmic debt and infernal lifeform by performing evil actions that increase karmic debt."

"But I still don't know which lifeform my soul will transmigrate to in the next life."

"It is difficult to determine the next lifeform as we cannot quantify karmic debt. We only know that the larger the karmic debt at death the less advanced the next lifeform. If you want to be a human being in the next life, you must perform, on average, more good than evil actions."

"I am wondering whether insects, and other subhuman beings can discriminate between good and evil actions. If not, how do they advance up the hierarchy?"

"The advancement up the hierarchy requires reduction in karmic debt, which can be achieved by picking the favorable environmental factors. Subhuman beings are not judicious and do not have discretion to choose the environmental factors; they must make use of the environmental factors available to them by coincidence. Their karmic debt will go down if by coincidence they are endowed with favorable environmental factors. We as human beings should be very careful not to increase our karmic debt to reach that situation where it takes uncontrollable time to come back as human beings."

"Many animals (if not most) eat other animals/creatures to survive — it seems that that's the way Nature operates. Are these animals increasing their karmic debt when they do so? If so, how do they ever evolve into a more advanced lifeform?"

"Jason, your question tells me that you are unable to identify the favorable environmental factors that help to decrease the karmic debt. Let me explain it with an example of carnivorous wolves. Like all living beings, wolves have basic survival instincts of food and possession. They worry about possession of food when there is scarcity of food. The intensity of their *moha* during conditions of food shortage is higher than that during conditions of food abundance. A wolf living in favorable environmental conditions, where there is plenty of food available, performs actions of killing with the intensity of *moha* that is less than the average intensity of *moha* of the karmic debt. Such an action of killing is a good action that reduces the accumulated karmic debt. Though the new action of killing creates karmic debt, its net effect is reduction in the karmic debt of the past actions. Does it make sense?"

"I never thought of it that way. Wow. Wolves can't control whether their environment is favorable for food or scare... so it's just up to chance, whether a wolf increases or decreases its karmic debt?"

"Jason, your inference is correct that subhuman beings can advance up the hierarchy by chance as favorable environmental conditions are endowed by chance. It may take them many reincarnations before reincarnating as a human being."

"Well, that's a clear enough explanation." I think to myself that Guru has answered most of my questions, but it feels like it's all swimming around in my head right now. Yet, my understanding of the karma doctrine is definitely taking shape. It does seem to be more logical and comprehensive than any other religious doctrine I've encountered.

"Jason, we have pretty much covered the basics of the karma doctrine. Of course, there is much more detail to the doctrine that we can discuss later if you want. But now we are ready to put the doctrine to the test by applying it to explain any unresolved questions you have. Is there anything on your mind that we need to address?"

"Yes. First, are all our actions determined? And if so, in what way can we be said to have free will?"

"The doctrine of free will is based on a presupposition that human beings are free to perform actions to fulfill the ambitions of their life. Is this proposition valid according to karmic doctrine? The validity of the proposition depends on whether our future actions are fully controlled by karma from our past actions. If they are, then we are not responsible for our actions and do not deserve retribution nor reward for them, which makes the karma doctrine meaningless. Only if we have some ability to choose our actions is the karma doctrine meaningful. We will examine the role of the karma doctrine in free will on Monday. In the meantime, you can read about free will on the Internet."

I leave Guru's abode for the library to read about free will, thinking about it as I drive. Though human beings are free to make efforts to fulfill their ambitions, I don't think the doctrine of free will, in itself, has anything to say about whether they will be able to fulfill their ambitions. I understand that my present actions must be partly controlled, but not fully controlled, by my past karma. I need to understand the factors, other than past karma, that control my present actions. Maybe my reading will help me understand or at least help me formulate my questions more clearly. I hope.

Chapter 12

Free Will

I decide to take two strenuous hikes in Yellowstone this weekend. Saturday, I hike to Avalanche Peak, a favorite hike of Yellowstone veterans. It's a steep hike through forests and wildflower meadows. I see amazing views that stretch across Yellowstone Lake, the Tetons, and the Absaroka Range. On Sunday, I hike to Mount Washburn Trail, which has stunning mountain top views of the Grand Tetons, the iconic Old Faithful Geyser, and the Grand Canyon of Yellowstone. I even see some bighorn sheep, bison, and elk. It is good to get a break from my studies, but I also keep thinking about Guru's teachings. I ponder how intensely to appreciate all this beauty. Hmm. Now I'm ready to get back into it.

Though I've gone through the process of learning the metaphysical model of the karma doctrine, I'm not quite clear in my mind how much control karma has over my life and how much control I have over my own karma. My expectation is that today's discussion will clarify some of this. I arrive at Guru's dwelling with this expectation and take my seat.

"You seem to have some questions on your mind," Guru states.

I've been waiting for this moment and immediately raise my uncertainty about the role of karma in my life. "Do I have any freedom to control my actions, or am I just a pawn in the hands of invisible karma?"

"Jason, I had a hunch that you would ask such a question, as the subject of free will has been a vital issue since the beginning of philosophical thought. That is why I asked you yesterday to do some research on the topic of free will. Were you able to do that?"

"Yes, I was able to find an Internet website and prepare a summary on the topic of free will."

"Proceed."

I turn on my laptop, open the folder, and read. "The question of free will is whether a person has freedom to exercise control over his or her actions. The answer requires understanding whether free will can coexist with determinism. The word 'determinism' is defined as the view that all current and future events are caused by past events combined with laws of nature. There are mainly three schools of thought. The members of one group, called determinists, accept determinism and reject free will; the members of the second group, called non-determinists, accept free will and reject determinism; and the members of the third group, called compatibilists, maintain that free will is consistent with some version of determinism or 'near' determinism."

"Jason, do you have any opinion on this issue?"

"I understand that, according to the karma doctrine, our present actions are at least partially controlled by karma that delivers the karmic consequences of our past actions. In other words, our present actions are at least partially caused by our past actions. The karma doctrine is based on the cause and effect law of nature, which asserts that every action has consequences, and the doer of the action bears the consequences of their actions. Therefore, determinism exists. But I also see that I have some freedom to exercise control over my actions and decisions. I pick my food, my clothes, my friends, and lots of other things. I myself made the final decision to attend Stanford University. If only the karma of my past actions has control over my present actions, then I shouldn't have any free will. How do I reconcile this contradiction?"

"You have a valid point. The development of an unconditional faith in the karma doctrine necessitates resolving the dilemma between free will and determinism. We will examine the role played by your karma in your admission to Stanford University. For our discussion we will first review the facts related to the process which led to your admission to Stanford University. How did you come to know about Stanford University?"

"I've visited Stanford University campus many times since it's very close to my hometown," I reply.

"Is the location of Stanford University your reason for attending it?"

"It's not the only reason. Stanford University is one of the top institutions in the world. My parents and my high school guidance counselor recommended it to me."

"Does your guidance counselor recommend this university to every student?"

"I don't think so. Only top students get admission to this university."

"You must be one of the top students?"

"Yes, I am."

"Are there any other requirements to get admission to this university?"

"One should score a high ranking on the SAT exam and also excel in extracurricular activities."

"Is there any financial requirement?"

"The tuition there is fairly high. Unless you either receive a scholarship or have well-to-do parents, it's very difficult to get admission."

"Are you going to get a scholarship?"

"No, my parents are going to support me."

"Your parents must be doing well financially."

"I'm fortunate in that respect."

"Did you apply for admission to other institutions?"

"I applied to four universities and was accepted by all of them, then chose Stanford because it seemed to be the best of the four."

"We now know the reasons for your selection of, and admission to, Stanford University. We will examine the role played by your karma in these reasons one by one. One of the reasons you selected Stanford University was its proximity to your home. Do you think your karma played any role in this?"

"I don't think so. My karma can't control the distance between my house and Stanford University."

"You have been admitted because your parents are willing to support you financially. How does your karma affect the wealth of your parents?"

"You've taught me that karma has no control over anyone's wealth, as wealth is an environmental consequence."

"Why did you take the SAT examination?"

"It was one of the requirements for admission."

"Did your karma cause you to take this exam?"

"I don't see any such mechanism."

"Can you identify any factor that was controlled by your karma and was one of the causes for your admission?"

"My understanding is that my intelligence is controlled by both knowledge-obscuring karma and will power that is controlled by spiritual-power-obscuring karma. The manifestation of these types of karma within me must be less intense in comparison to other students who didn't apply or didn't get admitted."

"Did your intelligence and will power play any role in your performance on the SAT examination?"

"I guess so. I was confident that I'd perform well on the exam."

"You chose Stanford University at the recommendation of your parents and guidance counselor. Do you think they made such a recommendation because of your karma?"

"Perhaps my karmic consequences, including my intelligence and will power to do well in life, affected their thinking."

"Excellent, Jason. You can see that, though many factors are not controlled by your karma, these factors and karma both affect you."

"Guru, I'm confused. I thought only karmic consequences affect me by changing the modes of the properties of my soul and body. So, how do all these factors that aren't controlled by my karma affect me? I understand that I must bear the karmic consequences of my past actions. Yet, it appears that I bear consequences other than the karmic. How does this work?"

"What does your experience in your daily life tell you?"

"According to my experience, I also experience the effects of others' actions, as well as natural events."

"Can you present some examples?"

"Yes, I can provide situations at different levels of social and political structures and from natural events. For example, my father made lots of money in stocks a few years back, which affected all the members of my family, including me. Also, the economic condition of my city is very healthy, primarily due to the hard work of our mayor, and this has a positive financial effect on those who live in the city. Another example is that lots of people in India recently benefited from globalization trends, like outsourcing of jobs from the USA. In all these cases many human beings experienced consequences of other people's actions. In addition, we experience effects such as the loss of personal belongings due to natural events like floods, fires, earthquakes, and the loss of life in accidents."

"Jason, it is obvious from the examples you just presented that the consequences of others' actions and natural events do influence us. I do not see anything wrong with your conclusion."

"But I do. If others' actions have control over me, then I'm not the master of my destiny. Suppose I want to achieve liberation from the cycle of reincarnation. Others can prevent me from doing so. I want to understand the karmic process through which I experience the effects of others' actions and natural events, but they don't have control over my destiny."

"Jason, I see your dilemma. Most of us face this quandary, because we fail to recognize that karmic consequences are not exclusively controlled by karma. Karma cannot deliver its consequences without the help of environmental factors."

"I'm afraid I don't understand the logic behind your statement."

"We have discussed this earlier but I need to explain it again for today's discussion. Three processes—performance of actions, fruition of past karma, and attachment of new karma—occur simultaneously in all living beings. For example, you are currently performing the action of participating in our discourse on the karma doctrine, attaching new karma to your karmic body, and bearing the karmic consequences of your past karma. The last process is changing the modes of the properties of your soul and body."

"But I'm not clear what your role is in changing the modes of my soul and body."

"The role of my action is to assist you in performing the current action of participating in our discourse on the karma doctrine. You could not perform the current action without my assistance and other means, such as my dwelling, a region, and time for conducting the discourse. The environmental factors, that include these means and my action, are the causes of the karmic consequences. Thus, there are two causes of the karmic consequences—fruition of karma and the environmental factors. Are both causes of the karmic consequences controlled by the karma doctrine?"

"No, only fruition of karma is controlled by the karma doctrine."

I am interrupted by my cell phone ringing. I apologize to Guru and answer the phone.

"Jason here. How can I help you?"

"This is Jim, the Park Ranger from Yellowstone National Park. Are you camping at Yellowstone?"

"Yes. Is there a problem?"

"Did you leave a bag full of groceries outside your tent after cooking outside this morning?"

"I did cook this morning. I'm normally very careful not to leave anything outside my tent. Can you tell me what happened?"

"Apparently you forgot the grocery bag outside your tent, and it attracted the attention of a grizzly bear. I expect you can imagine the fate of your bag. Please be careful in the future not to leave any food item outside your tent."

"I'm sorry for the negligence. I'll definitely be more careful in the future not to leave anything outside my tent."

"Good day, Jason."

"Good day and thank you, Jim."

I normally put my cell phone on silent every day before the start of our discussion. It seems I forgot to do that today. This is a bad day for my memory. I guess I was too anxious to have this discussion about free will. I apologize to Guru for the interruption. Guru's reaction to the interruption surprises me. Instead of being disturbed by the interruption, Guru is pleased with it.

"Jason, I am happy with the event of this interruption, as I can use it to explain the karmic process through which the effects of others' actions are experienced and the concept of free will. Let us compare the nature of your action and the nature of the change in your knowledge before and during the interruption. Was the nature of your action before interruption different than that during the interruption?"

"I think so. Before the interruption, the physical actions of my body, speech, and mind and the psychic actions driven by my ego were different than that during the interruption. I was conversing with you face to face before interruption, while I was talking to Jim on the cell phone during the interruption."

"Was the nature of the change in your knowledge different during the two periods?"

"Yes. The state of my knowledge of the karma doctrine

was changing before the interruption, while the change in my knowledge during the interruption had nothing to do with karma doctrine."

"Both my action of participating in the discussion on the karma doctrine and Jim's action of talking about the incident at the campsite affected the modes of your soul and body. Do you have some sense of the process through which others' actions affect you?"

"I think I now understand the karmic process through which I experience the effect of others' actions. The karmic consequences depend not only on fruition of karma but also on environmental factors. Since the environmental factors before and during the interruption were different, the karmic consequences before and during the interruption were different. Others' actions affect me indirectly through karmic consequences."

"Keep in mind that though we are emphasizing only the changes in the modes in your action and knowledge as the karmic consequences, the modes of all four properties of your soul and four properties of your body are changing due to fruition of all seven types of karmas concurrently. And not only my and Jim's actions, but other environmental conditions around you also are serving as efficient causes of the karmic consequences. Now you know the effect of others' actions on the karmic process. But what can you say about free will?"

"Apparently, I have the freedom to pick efficient causes of karmic consequences. Using my free will, I decided to answer the cell phone, which was picking an efficient cause of the karmic consequences in this situation."

"Jason, as a matter of fact, the only thing we do all our life is pick efficient causes of karmic consequences. We pick our food, our clothes, our friends, and our foes. We pick the entertainment programs we watch, the books we read, the discourses we listen to, and the work we do. We recall past experiences, feelings, ideas, viewpoints, and beliefs from our memory for analyzing current events. All these different things, which we pick every day of our lives, serve as efficient causes of karmic consequences. For example, the food we eat is an efficient cause of the karmic consequence of the physique-determining karma; the book we read is an efficient cause of the karmic consequence of the knowledge-obscuring karma; and the past way of thinking we use to evaluate current happenings is an efficient cause of the nature-deluding and power-determining karmas. The efficient causes we choose with our free will affect our new actions. By selecting a desirable efficient cause of karmic consequences, we can perfect our new actions. Because we have the freedom to select the efficient causes of karmic consequences, we are morally responsible for our actions. The karma doctrine would become meaningless if our actions were completely determined by our past actions. If it is a misconception that our new actions are completely determined by our past actions, is karma doctrine deterministic?"

"It doesn't seem so."

"The karmic process appears to be non-deterministic because present actions are not completely determined by past actions. However, once a person exercises free will to choose an efficient cause of karmic consequences, the causal conditions (fruition of karma and environmental factors) are enough to cause him to act in a certain manner. This means that the karmic process is 'near' deterministic, not 'strictly' deterministic. We do choose the environmental factors of our actions, but within a constraint. Jason, I hope that today's discussion helped you to address some of your questions about free will."

"Yes. It did help me, but how do you define this constraint?"

"I am pleased to hear that today's discussion helped you to understand the concept of free will, but I need to elaborate the constraint in choosing the environmental factors of our actions. There are countless environmental factors in the universe, but not every environmental factor is a potential efficient cause of the karmic consequences in any one situation. Only those environmental factors which are accessible to a person are potential efficient causes of karmic consequences for that person. For example, if a person lives in a country where no Jain saint comes to visit, then the means of listening to the discourse of a Jain saint cannot be a potential environmental factor of his action. Another example is that several environmental factors are not accessible to persons in prison. A prisoner cannot pick his food, clothes, friends, and foes outside of the prison, certain entertainment programs to watch and books to read, etc. Are you with me, Jason?"

"Yes, I now understand that the constraint in choosing environmental factors has to do with accessibility, but I have another question. Isn't my response—physically and emotionally—to my chosen environmental factors also an act of free will?"

"Once you exercise your free will to choose the environmental factors of karmic consequences, these causal conditions are enough to determine the karmic consequences, including your response. You have no control over your response to the chosen efficient cause. Your new action, physical as well as psychic, which is one of the components of your karmic consequences, is determined. For example, once you chose Jim's statement as the efficient cause, you had no control over your new action. Tell me what was going through your mind when you were listening to Jim's statement."

"I was trying to ascertain whether Jim made a mistake, because I've always been careful not to leave any food items outside my tent. But then I thought about my belief that most civil servants are trustworthy persons. My answer to Jim's statement was based on this belief."

"Once you chose your interpretation of Jim's statement, it served as the efficient cause of your next new action that was determined; you had no control over your response to Jim's statement."

"That doesn't make sense to me. If I wanted, I could have said to Jim that he was mistaken because I didn't leave any grocery bag outside my tent."

"I agree. You could have done that."

"If so, then my action is not determined."

"Your action is determined for a chosen efficient cause. Had you chosen a different efficient cause, your action would have been different."

"I don't understand."

"If you had a belief that civil servants' statements are not to be believed, you would not have picked Jim's statement as the efficient cause. Instead you would have picked the statement 'do not believe civil servants' as the efficient cause, and your response would have been different, such as 'I did not leave the grocery bag outside my tent.'"

"I now understand that my response is controlled by the fruition of karma and the chosen environmental factors as efficient cause, but I have another question. I sometimes feel that the environmental factors are given to me rather my choosing them. For example, I am unable to control my mind during meditation. It wanders around either remembering various past events or planning various future actions. There are many nights when I cannot fall asleep for several hours because my mind keeps brooding about various issues. I don't think I am picking these issues myself."

"Most of us have stored many past events and future plans in our memory which serve as an efficient cause of loss of concentration of mind either during meditation or sleeping hours. The loss of concentration of mind, either during meditation or sleeping hours, is not considered as denial of free will, since many people are able, and hence free, to control their mind under pressure.

"So, when you say that you are not picking the environmental factors, it is your ego that is controlling you. The only way to gain control of your ego is to reduce your karmic debt.

"Jason, I hope that today's discussion helped you to answer some of your questions about free will."

"Yes, it did help me. I now understand that the doctrine of free will has to be valid, as new actions are not completely determined by past actions."

"I am pleased to hear that. We have covered most of the basic concepts of the karma doctrine. Do you want me to discuss any other topic in our next discourse?"

"Most people desire wealth, health, and happiness. Is fulfilment of such a desire consistent with the karma doctrine?"

"This is indeed a good topic for our next discourse. See you tomorrow. Could you do some reading on the immune system on the Web for tomorrow?"

I bow to Guru and leave for the campsite.

Chapter 13

Health, Wealth, and Happiness

Wouldn't it be wonderful if everyone in the world were healthy, wealthy, and happy? Can knowledge of the karma doctrine provide a path to these conditions? I already know that wealth is not controlled by the karma doctrine. Since it's hard to be happy without wealth, is happiness not controlled by the karma doctrine, either? And what about health? Is the effect of a virus, like coronavirus, on one's health directed by the karma doctrine? Suddenly, I hear Guru's voice.

"Jason, wake up. Where are you? What are you thinking?"

I open my eyes and find myself sitting on my usual seat in Guru's dwelling. I've been so engrossed in trying to relate happiness to karma that I don't even remember when I arrived here.

"I'm sorry, Guru. Did you ask me something?"

"You are clearly engrossed in something. What is it?"

"You're right. I'm wondering if or how health, wealth, and happiness are related to the karma doctrine. I think that we surely need some money to meet our daily needs, and hence, our needs for happiness. But since wealth isn't controlled by the karma doctrine, I guess happiness also isn't controlled by the karma doctrine. Right?"

"Before discussing whether happiness is governed by the karma doctrine or not, let me ask you one hypothetical question. If an angel granted you one gift, what would you ask for— health, wealth, or happiness?"

"I'd ask for wealth, because I could basically buy the means of health and happiness with wealth."

"Most people, including you, operate from ego. Due to ego, they identify health and happiness with wealth, because they equate health and happiness with what they can acquire with wealth. For most young Americans, happiness means the American dream. They dream of a day when everyone will have plenty of food to eat, enough clothes to wear, and a modern residence with lots of high-tech facilities. These people ignore the fact that even those people who have achieved the American dream are not happy all the time. People care about their bodies because they wrongly equate self to their body, not soul. Therefore, they believe the body is most pertinent to happiness."

"I don't understand this wrong equation you are talking about. Can you elaborate?"

"If you look for an object in the wrong location, you cannot find it. For example, you will not be able to locate consciousness if you look for it in an inanimate object. Why? Because consciousness is a property of soul, not of matter. Similarly, happiness is an intrinsic property of soul, not of body. You cannot find happiness in the body because it is not there. It is experienced only by soul, either indirectly, using the body, including senses and mind as the medium, or directly, without the help of any medium. The former is superficial happiness, which we will call physical happiness. The latter is real happiness, which we previously termed inner peace. We do not need to be wealthy to attain inner peace because the consequences of actions that create wealth and actions that create inner peace are governed by different laws. While inner peace is governed by the law of karma, wealth is controlled by man-made laws. All of us experience episodes of physical happiness in our daily lives, but very few of us have experienced inner peace. Due to the misbelief that the body, not the soul, is most pertinent to happiness, we remain so engrossed in achieving superficial happiness that we do not allow glimpses of real happiness."

"To me, physical happiness is real. I feel happy wearing nice clothes, eating tasty foods, smelling pleasant odors, watching entertaining programs, and listening to my favorite music."

"Actually, physical happiness does not lie in all these objects of enjoyment you mentioned. If it did, everyone should feel happy to get these objects. But that is not the case. The clothes and food and other material things that give pleasure to you will not necessarily make others happy. The primary cause of happiness or misery is never the means of happiness or misery but your thoughts about it. For example, a person owns and lives in a moderate size house that is flanked by a mansion on the right side and a hut on the left side. He feels unhappy whenever he sees the mansion on the right, but he is happy seeing the hut on the left. One can argue that physical happiness is not real. It is temporary and depends on your thinking, the imagination of your mind. On the other hand, real happiness—inner peace—is experienced directly by the soul."

"Are you suggesting that one should renounce the means of physical happiness to achieve real happiness?"

"We already have real happiness/inner peace, as it is an intrinsic property of our soul, but it is defiled by our *moha*. We barely experience inner peace because the intensity of our *moha* remains high most of the time. Due to the high intensity of *moha*, our attachment to means of physical happiness and our aversion to means of misery are intense. What one needs to do is renounce the attachment to means of physical happiness and the aversion to means of misery, not the means of happiness and misery themselves. Both the intensity of inner peace, and the intensity of attachment or aversion to means of physical happiness or misery, vary with the intensity of *moha*, but in an opposite manner. While the intensity of inner peace increases with a decrease in *moha*, the intensity of attachment and aversion increases with an increase in *moha*. And remember intensity of *moha* relates directly to karmic debt. When *moha's* intensity increases, karmic debt increases; when *moha's* intensity decreases, karmic debt decreases."

"It seems that karmic debt is the critical parameter for real happiness, but how do I know what my karmic debt is?"

"Since the karmic body is made of subtle matter that is too fine to be detected by available scientific tools, karmic debt cannot be known. However, you can estimate your current karmic debt by assessing the intensity of your existing *moha*, which primarily consists of ego and the four negative passions of anger, pride, deceit, and greed. Ego and the negative passions are highly correlated; if ego is intense, so are negative passions. Only you yourself, through self-examination, can assess the intensity of your ego, unless it is so high that others can easily identify you as a highly egoistic person. There are some core factors that serve as indicators of ego, such as harboring grievances, needing to be right, having to win, feeling superior, and seeking fame. Those who have most of these signs have intense ego, and hence large karmic debt. The first step in ego assessment is to have awareness of it, which we do not have without intentional and honest self-examination. However, the knowledge of karmic debt is not as important as the knowledge of the type of actions that reduce karmic debt."

"How does one reduce his or her karmic debt?"

"We have discussed this earlier, Jason. Does the term nonviolent actions ring a bell for you?"

"Oh, yes; I remember now. One needs to perform nonviolent actions to reduce one's karmic debt. While most violent actions involve intense *moha*, and hence increase karmic debt, nonviolent actions are carried out with mild *moha*, and they reduce karmic debt."

"Can you identify one type of violent action that is carried out by most people who belong to the upper strata of society?"

"No, I need your help to answer that question."

"Any action that hurts others is a violent action. Actions performed by upper strata people to acquire more than their fair share of natural resources are violent actions, because they cause suffering to people of lower strata."

"So, suffering in the world could be diminished by reducing the income inequality in society. No wonder people in Scandinavian countries seem to live with less tension in their lives. When we first started talking today, acquiring wealth seemed like a natural path to happiness, but now I see that wealth provides only superficial happiness and even results in violence to others. And only nonviolent actions can lead to real happiness and realization of inner peace.

"Okay, let's consider health," I say. "I have a philosophical question. Why can't we have a disease-free world?"

"A disease-free world sounds nice, but it would actually be a chaotic world. In a disease-free world, people could live any lifestyle, eat whatever they want and as much as they want, and they would still be healthy. No diet or eating habits would be unhealthy. Since people would never die from diseases, some of them would have to be killed by violence to feed the surviving population because natural resources would be insufficient. Therefore, it seems logical to assume that disease manifestation is nature's way of maintaining an orderly world."

"What about health conditions?" I ask. "Does karmic debt also affect our health?"

"Our health is controlled by the physique-determining karma, which in turn is affected by the karmic debt we carry at any moment. Karmic debt keeps fluctuating up and down, depending on the nature of our actions, which includes *moha*, hence negative passions. Intense *moha* means intense negative passions, which affect the immune systems of our bodies. With increasing negative passions, our immune system becomes weak, and we increasingly become unhealthy. Jason, can you summarize the information on the immune system that you gathered on the Web?"

"Sure, Guru." I open the file on my laptop and read, "Our immune system protects our body against disease or other potentially damaging foreign bodies such as viruses, bacteria, and parasites. There are two major subsystems of the immune system: the innate immune system and the adaptive immune system. The innate immune system provides an immediate, but non-specific, response to all threats. The adaptive immune response is antigen-specific and requires the recognition of specific 'non-self' antigens. The innate immune system is the dominant system of immune defense. If pathogens successfully evade the innate response, the adaptive immune system, which is a second defense mechanism, is activated by the innate response. Adaptive immunity creates immunological memory after an initial response to a specific pathogen, leading to an enhanced response to subsequent encounters with that same pathogen. This process of acquired immunity is the basis of vaccination."

"You have done a nice job of presenting the information on the immune system, Jason. Two of the subtypes of the physique-determining karma relevant to health are organ-appendage and immune-suppressing karmas. The organ-appendage karma causes the origin and maintenance of the organs and their appendages, and the immune-suppressing karma determines the potency of immunity. Karmic debt, fed by *moha,* controls the functional efficiency of the organs and their appendages, including the potency of immunity, but all organs are not affected equally by *moha*. The organs that are extra affected by *moha* are determined by environmental factors. For example, while the organs related to the pulmonary system are more affected by cigarette smoking, the organs related to the digestive system are more affected by sedentary behavior. Karmic consequences are controlled by the combination of karma and environmental factors. The functional efficiency of these subsystems of the immune system varies from person to person and from birth to death."

"Who has a strong immune system?"

"The few people who performed their actions, both in previous lives and in this life, with mild *moha* are born with robust immune systems that remain efficient until death. They live a tension-free life and stay healthy throughout their lives."

"Doesn't the immune system become weak with age?"

"Most people are born with an efficient immune system that becomes more inefficient with aging due to inappropriate daily conduct. Such people eventually get infected by diseases and may die from those diseases. Though such people had performed their actions in the previous lives with mild *moha*, leading to birth with an efficient immune system, they performed their actions in the present life with increasing *moha*."

"Okay. So, who is born with a weak immune system?"

"Some people's immune systems are weak at birth. These people suffer from chronic diseases and often eventually die from them. Such people performed their actions with strong *moha* both in their previous and present lives. However, even those who are born with a weak immune system can improve their immune system by performing actions according to righteous conduct."

"I now understand the reasons to follow righteous conduct, but it isn't clear to me whether infection by a virus like Covid-19 is due to karmic debt."

"Any disease, including Covid-19 infection, is the result of the karmic consequences of the organ-appendage and immune-suppressing karmas. However, we have talked about the fact that karmic consequences depend not only on karma, but also on environmental factors that are not governed by the karma doctrine. Covid-19 infection, for example, could be avoided by following the protocols laid down by the health department. Though the statement that the Covid-19 infection of a group of people is due to their past karma is true, it does not convey the complete truth. The incomplete truth gives the notion that people have no ability to prevent it, which is not correct.

Choosing to follow recommended protocols might prevent it. That is an environmental factor."

"I learned a lot today. I can maintain a strong immune system, thus preventing diseases, by following righteous nonviolent conduct that reduces karmic debt. That conduct will also lead to real happiness, not just the superficial happiness of wealth, and a more peaceful life. Based on our previous discussions, I understand this conduct will also lead to a better lifeform in the next life. Cool!"

"Jason, I am very impressed with your enthusiasm for learning the karma doctrine. The next discourse is going to be your final chance to ask any questions you still have on the karma doctrine. I expect that you have many questions on the karma doctrine because you were raised by a family that did not believe in it. Also, I would like to hear your views about our discourse. That would be helpful in improving how I teach the doctrine in the future. And I would like to conclude our final discourse with some remarks on spiritual growth."

I bow my head and leave for the campsite to think about what I see as the weaknesses and strengths of the karma doctrine.

Chapter 14

Steps toward Spiritual Growth

Time flies when you're engaged in something that fascinates you so much. I can't believe that I've already attended twelve sessions with Guru. Today's my last meeting with him. I'm happy that the discussion will be over today because I was becoming oversaturated with information and ideas to think about. But I also learned a lot from it, and I now have a very different perspective on the purpose of life. I arrive at Guru's dwelling with mixed feelings about the adventure. Guru greets me with folded hands. His gesture surprises me, as he has never done this before.

"Jason, I see you are surprised by me greeting you this way," remarks Guru as I take my seat.

"That's true."

"Jason, you were my pupil until yesterday. Today you are my equal. I hope that you learned something worthwhile from our discourse. Today is your last chance to ask questions on the karma doctrine."

"I do have a number of questions. I grew up in a family whose religion depended on divine revelation as the foundation. Since that's not possible in this version of the karma doctrine, with no supreme being, where did this theory come from? How is it possible that a doctrine of such intricacy was discovered so many centuries ago?"

"Knowledge of the karma doctrine was not acquired by sensory- and mind-based knowledge or language-based verbal knowledge, our standard ways of learning. Instead, such knowledge was revealed many centuries ago by an omniscient, someone who became omniscient upon completely liquidating their karmic debt."

"Can you name this person?"

"His name was Mahavira, and he re-established the ancient religion of Jainism in the 6th century BC."

"Oh, yes, now I remember reading about Mahavira in a book about Jainism my friend Ajay loaned me. He was a monk and a contemporary of Gautama Buddha."

"Yes."

"So if I understand correctly, the karma doctrine in scriptures is presented as a set of statements that command unswerving faith, but these statements can't be proven. The karma doctrine discovered in our discussions is also based on several presuppositions that can't be proven. Why should one have faith in these presuppositions, Guru?"

"The scriptures are written in a traditional 'top-down' approach in which perfect knowledge, which is the highest type of knowledge that cannot be wrong, is the source of information. But in the present scientific age, one cannot have faith in the karma doctrine without examining it from a scientific viewpoint, with the touchstone of logic and reasoning. You and I discovered the model of the karma doctrine using a different approach, called a 'bottom-up' approach. In a bottom-up approach, lower types of knowledge, which are susceptible to error and are acquired with the help of senses, mind, and language, are the source of information. In the bottom-up approach, we followed a scientific procedure in which a set of presuppositions were first established, and the presuppositions, along with logic, were used to discover the karma doctrine. The presuppositions allowed the model based on them to explain the phenomena under consideration. There is hardly any need for 'blind faith' in the bottom-up approach."

"Okay. Here's another question. It's hard to conceive of something with no beginning and no end, when fossil records tell us lots of stories of beginnings and endings. Aren't those contradictory ideas?"

"It is the substances that constitute living beings that are assumed to be uncreated and eternal, not the shape and size of living bodies. The shape and size of the body depend on the karmic consequences of the physique-determining karma, which is in turn controlled by both karma's fruition and environmental factors. As environmental factors are neither eternal nor uncreated, neither are the shape and size of living beings. There are many creatures, such as dinosaurs, that no longer exist due to different environmental factors. However, the substances that make up living beings are uncreated and eternal."

"That clarification helps. Here's another thing I've been wondering about. If the karma doctrine is so rational, why isn't it accepted by more people?"

"All of us, except a handful people, carry a large karmic debt. Our ego is so intense that we have a false belief that we are made of body only and do not pay any attention to our soul. We have either incorrect information about, or are ignorant of, the karma doctrine and thus think of it as nothing but a heap of imaginary ideas."

"What would you advise to those who have a common feeling that it's enough to worry about our current lifetime—that if we start worrying about our prior lives or future lives, it will be overwhelming?"

"I believe in the principle of non-absolutism. According to this principle, truth has multiple facets. We know only a few facets of truth and we believe in those facets of truth. Others also know only a few facets of truth that may be different than ours, and they believe in those facets of truth. There we must recognize the fact that everybody knows only partial facets of truth. We should not force others to accept our known facets of truth. Everyone should try to find as many facets of truth as possible and follow the most appealing one(s)."

"Oh. Well, my ego is telling me to quit, so I have no more

questions on the karma doctrine."

"I can understand your state of mind, but you can help me. I would like to know your views about the discourse because your comments will be helpful to me in planning my future teaching."

"Guru, your request creates a dilemma for me. I don't want to tell a lie, and I don't want to hurt you by telling the truth."

"You could follow the course taken by a saintly person when a hunter asked him the direction in which his prey ran away. The saintly person did not want to get the prey killed by telling the truth and he did not want to tell a lie either."

"What did he do?"

"He kept silent. The hunter left him alone thinking that he was deaf. Had the hunter convinced the saintly person that he was not going to hurt the prey, the saintly person would have told him the truth. I can assure you that your true views about the discourse are not going to hurt my feelings."

"Okay. I started out with an entirely different notion about the nature of the answers the karma doctrine would provide. My notion was based on a book I read earlier on this topic. The book was easy to read but had very little substance. It was very general in nature, with few specifics. Most concepts were so vague that it was difficult for me to summarize what I read. I was expecting a similar type of vague answer. That's why I was a little perplexed in the first few discussions. I soon realized that the answers I was going to receive in these discussions would be miles apart from what I expected."

"Did you have a notion of karma before coming here?"

"Yes, I had some vague notion what karma is all about. But I now realize that all my ideas about karma were so heavily flawed that I might as well discard them altogether. I can understand why you didn't use the word karma in the early discussions. You didn't want me to get the idea that the metaphysical model is another version of the commonly accepted concepts of karma."

"What are the appealing aspects of the model, in your opinion?"

"The model is based on logic, not on any religious dogmas. It doesn't invoke any mystical, supernatural power, like God, and doesn't demand the application of mystical techniques. Most of the concepts in the model have a scientific basis."

"Why do you think that the model is not based on any religion?"

"I don't recall that you mentioned any religion during the discourse, except that you studied Jainism to develop the metaphysical model."

"Jason, your recollection is correct; we did not bring up any religion in our discourses. Our metaphysical model does not include any statement that requires reference to some luminous spiritual magnet. It is a model that is based on eternal and universal laws; hence, the model is applicable to every living being. I should mention, however, that during my study of eastern religions I discovered that Jain canons include the most detailed description of the karma doctrine. Now tell me the least appealing aspect of the model."

"The model is impractical to follow in daily life."

"Jason, I had a hunch you would say that. Which aspect of the model do you think is impractical?"

"The model demands complete renunciation of physical objects, which is almost impossible in everyday life."

"Complete renunciation is required for achieving liberation. Only exceptional individuals seek liberation. Most people seek happiness in the moment. Lasting happiness can be achieved by minimizing one's desires and, in turn, minimizing attachment to physical objects. The model demands detachment from, not renunciation of, physical objects. Since detachment from physical objects is difficult without renouncing them, it is desirable to minimize their importance gradually. The importance of physical objects gradually and automatically diminishes as one advances on the spiritual path. The model delineates a path that ends in liberation. One cannot get there without traveling on the path. One should travel on the path at his or her own pace. It is always difficult to take the first step. As one gets familiar with the path, the journey on it becomes easier. As one advances on the spiritual journey, he or she gains sufficient spiritual energy to recognize his or her own personal path with ever increasing clarity. Does this make any sense to you?"

"I understand what you're saying. I need more time to contemplate the model, as I belong to a religion that does not believe in reincarnation."

"Now that you have discovered the karma model, the question might arise, what can I do with it? Now you have a few models: the familiar materialistic model, the traditional religious model founded on worship of deity, and the newly discovered alternative karma model. The karma model offers you an alternative view regarding how life functions. It gives you awareness to everlasting inner peace. Life is and becomes what we believe. For a while, conduct your daily routine using both models—what can you lose? Keep in mind that each of us has the potential to achieve everlasting inner peace by liquidating our karmic debt with our own effort. Always remember the golden rule that spiritual growth is achieved by conducting nonviolent actions that reduce karmic debt. Spiritual growth leads to the destruction of ego, the change in our attitude toward life and outlook toward worldly objects, and the realization that the soul is the location of inner peace. Every person should devise their daily conduct to reduce karmic debt for achieving spiritual growth. The following suggestions can be helpful in developing the daily routine:

Take initiative. Do not procrastinate and use the excuse, 'I am too busy.' What can be more important than having inner peace in your life? It should not be hard to give up debilitating shows on social media for about thirty minutes and devote that time instead to activities for spiritual development. Gradually reduce the time for watching meaningless shows and increase the time and priority for spiritual activities.

Be a vegetarian/vegan. Living a vegetarian/vegan life is not only nonviolent and sound for your body and mind, it is beneficial also for the environment. It is the only way to sustain the ever-increasing population of the world. View a few documentaries that explain the personal and global effects of this eating lifestyle. Vegetarian meals can be more delicious than nonvegetarian meals if you know how to cook them properly. Try not eating any animal products for a period of two to three weeks and then feel the difference in your outlook. Once you pass this test, you will become vegetarian/vegan forever.

Become aware of brief flashes of strange clarity. These flashes are indications of our potential of spiritual growth. The sooner you control your ego, the sooner you begin to experience transient spiritual awakening that eventually becomes a natural feature of your life.

Perform nonviolent deeds. Commit your full energy and capabilities to conducting nonviolent deeds. Slowly but steadily reduce your attachment to worldly possessions. For example, if you own ten shirts, give up the shirt to which you have the most attachment and manage with nine. Gradually, dissolve *moha*.

Be an efficient cause for nonviolent deeds. You can never be the material cause of others' deeds, but others can choose your deeds as the efficient cause of fruition of their karma. Conduct only such deeds which can be used by others as the efficient cause of fruition of their auspicious karma.

Contemplate. Introspect and self-analyze for self-reformation. Spend a few minutes each day to review your daily activities. Acknowledge your mistakes and resolve not to repeat them in the future. Contemplate that you are not the body and that you have potential of becoming a pure soul.

Be determined. Do not allow the 'initial fear' to run your conduct. As you advance on the spiritual path, you will acquire new insight to guide your future course of action."

"Guru, my time with you has been very fruitful to me. I must admit that I at first regretted my decision to accept your offer, but I was wrong. My outlook on life has changed remarkably. I promise you that I'll come back next year to learn some more details of the metaphysical model. And I can assure you that I'll further contemplate the model and try to perform nonviolent actions in my life."

"Jason, I am happy that you are willing to devote your time to contemplate the model and perform nonviolent actions. I will look forward to meeting you next year. You have been an excellent pupil and now you are a superb equal."

Guru folds his hands and wishes me good luck. I also fold my hands and bow my head to pay my respect to Guru. I depart with moist eyes and a new sense of responsibility but also with a very full heart.

Glossary

Action: Any physical, oral, or mental activity performed by *yoga*-plus-*moha* is an action, p. 61.

Advanced lifeform: Any physically and spiritually developed living being is an advanced lifeform. A living being with a greater number of senses, a mind, and greater spiritual growth is a more advanced lifeform, p. 123.

Belief-deluding karma: Fruition of this karma affects the innate ability to perceive truth and causes a false understanding of self—that "I" am the body—termed ego, p. 106.

Bondage: Karmic matter is bound to the karmic body through bondage, an extrinsic property of karmic matter, p. 74.

Decreased realization: The time and intensity of delivery of consequences of old karma are decreased by this extrinsic property of karmic matter, p. 96.

Efficient cause: That which does not change its own condition to bring about an effect is an efficient cause. The efficient cause itself cannot turn into the effect but does contribute to it, p. 52.

Ego: Essentially, ego is false belief regarding self. Humans generally do not discriminate between the soul and the body and have a misconception that "I" (my ego) am the body, p. 43.

Environmental consequences: These are the consequences of an action that are controlled by environmental factors and are non-universal, p. 65.

Environmental factors: Factors, including human-made laws, that change depending on time and place and impact consequences of actions, p. 65.

Feeling-determining karma: Fruition of this karma affects the performance of senses and is responsible for worldly experiences of misery and pleasure, pp. 83–84.

Immune-suppressing karma: Fruition of this karma affects functioning of the immune system, p. 88.

Increased realization: The time and intensity of delivery of consequences of old karma are increased by this extrinsic property of karmic matter, p. 96.

Karma: Karma is the living karmic matter of the karmic body which serves as a carrier and a deliverer of the directives for universal consequences of actions, p. 73.

Karmic body: Every living being has a karmic body made of karmic matter, p. 72.

Karmic consequences: These are the consequences of karma that manifest as new modes of the properties of soul and body, p. 85.

Karmic debt: A debt, in the form of karmic matter, attached to the karmic body for every action, that is to be liquidated in the future. This debt depends on the intensity of *moha*. The larger the intensity of *moha* of an action, the larger the karmic debt acquired during that action, pp. 81–82.

Karmic matter: The subtle matter that carries directives for the universal consequences of actions, pp. 71–72.

Knowledge-obscuring karma: Fruition of this karma obstructs the inherent knowledge of soul, so that only partial knowledge manifests in worldly souls, p. 82.

Lifespan-determining karma: This karma determines the duration of each embodiment, p. 84.

Living matter: Matter that has association with a soul, such as bodily matter, p. 27.

Material cause: That which changes its own condition to bring about an effect is a material cause. The effect is a potentiality in the material cause, p. 52.

Mode: The state of the properties of a substance that undergoes change, p. 16.

Moha: Ego, passions, and quasi-passions make up *moha*, an extrinsic property of soul, p. 44.

Nature-deluding karma: Fruition of this karma partly defiles the property of inner peace of soul with *moha*, causing the living being to not understand its true nature, p. 83.

Nonliving matter: Any matter other than living matter, p. 27.

Nonviolent action: An action governed by five types of abstinence: abstention from (1) harming or killing living beings, (2) false or hurtful speech, (3) theft and illegal or immoral transactions, (4) unchaste sexual acts, and (5) craving and hoarding worldly possessions, p. 112.

Passions and quasi-passions: There are four negative passions: anger, pride, deceit, and greed; and nine negative quasi-passions: gaiety, pleasure, displeasure, grief, fear, disgust; and sexual cravings of three types: male, female, and hermaphrodite. All of these are components of *moha*, p. 44.

Physical happiness: A sense of happiness that is experienced by the soul indirectly, using the body, including senses and mind as the medium, p. 145.

Physiological karma: Fruition of this karma affects the various physiological properties of body, p. 83.

Physiological properties: Sense, power, lifespan, and physique are the physiological properties of living beings, p. 37.

Physique-determining karma: Fruition of this karma affects a variety of physiological functions ranging from the realm of birth to the minutest details of the body, p. 84.

Power-determining karma: Fruition of this karma affects bodily movements, vocal expressions, and mental choices, p. 84.

Power restraint: Control over physical actions of the body, vocal organs, and mind requires power restraint, p. 120.

Psychical karma: Fruition of this karma affects the psychical properties of soul, p. 82.

Real happiness: Happiness that is experienced by soul directly, without the help of any medium, like senses, p. 145.

Righteous conduct: Conduct which diminishes the intensity of *yoga* and *moha*, p. 118.

Sense restraint: The practice of control over sense organs in order to decrease attachment to the body, p. 119.

Spiritual-power-obscuring karma: Fruition of this karma obstructs the inherent spiritual power of soul, so that only partial spiritual power manifests in worldly souls, p. 82.

Subtle matter: Matter that is too fine to be detected using available scientific equipment, p. 70.

Universal consequences: The principle that all consequences of actions that are governed by the karma doctrine are consistent regardless of the time and place of the actions, p. 63.

Universal law: Any law that is valid in all times and places, p. 62.

Yoga: Physical action of the body, vocal organs, and mind, p. 61.

MANTRA
BOOKS

EASTERN RELIGION & PHILOSOPHY

We publish books on Eastern religions and philosophies. Books
that aim to inform and explore the various traditions that began in
the East and have migrated West.
If you have enjoyed this book, why not tell other readers by
posting a review on your preferred book site.

Recent bestsellers from MANTRA BOOKS are:

The Way Things Are
A Living Approach to Buddhism
Lama Ole Nydahl
An introduction to the teachings of the Buddha, and how to make
use of these teachings in everyday life.
Paperback: 978-1-84694-042-2 ebook: 978-1-78099-845-9

Back to the Truth
5000 Years of Advaita
Dennis Waite
A demystifying guide to Advaita for both those new to, and those
familiar with this ancient, non-dualist philosophy from India.
Paperback: 978-1-90504-761-1 ebook: 978-184694-624-0

Shinto: A celebration of Life
Aidan Rankin
Introducing a gentle but powerful spiritual pathway reconnecting
humanity with Great Nature and affirming all aspects of life.
Paperback: 978-1-84694-438-3 ebook: 978-1-84694-738-4

In the Light of Meditation
Mike George
A comprehensive introduction to the practice of meditation and
the spiritual principles behind it. A 10 lesson meditation pro-
gramme with CD and internet support.
Paperback: 978-1-90381-661-5

A Path of Joy
Popping into Freedom
Paramananda Ishaya
A simple and joyful path to spiritual enlightenment.
Paperback: 978-1-78279-323-6 ebook: 978-1-78279-322-9

The Less Dust the More Trust
Participating in The Shamatha Project, Meditation and Science
Adeline van Waning, MD PhD
The inside-story of a woman participating in frontline meditation research, exploring the interfaces of mind-practice, science and psychology.
Paperback: 978-1-78099-948-7 ebook: 978-1-78279-657-2

I Know How To Live, I Know How To Die
The Teachings of Dadi Janki: A warm, radical, and life-affirming view of who we are, where we come from, and what time is calling us to do
Neville Hodgkinson
Life and death are explored in the context of frontier science and deep soul awareness.
Paperback: 978-1-78535-013-9 ebook: 978-1-78535-014-6

Living Jainism
An Ethical Science
Aidan Rankin, Kanti V. Mardia
A radical new perspective on science rooted in intuitive awareness and deductive reasoning.
Paperback: 978-1-78099-912-8 ebook: 978-1-78099-911-1

Ordinary Women, Extraordinary Wisdom
The Feminine Face of Awakening
Rita Marie Robinson
A collection of intimate conversations with female spiritual teachers who live like ordinary women, but are engaged with their true natures.
Paperback: 978-1-84694-068-2 ebook: 978-1-78099-908-1

The Way of Nothing
Nothing in the Way
Paramananda Ishaya
A fresh and light-hearted exploration of the amazing reality of
nothingness.
Paperback: 978-1-78279-307-6 ebook: 978-1-78099-840-4

Readers of ebooks can buy or view any of these bestsellers by
clicking on the live link in the title. Most titles are published in
paperback and as an ebook. Paperbacks are available in traditional
bookshops. Both print and ebook formats are available online.

Find more titles and sign up to our readers' newsletter at
http://www.johnhuntpublishing.com/mind-body-spirit.
Follow us on Facebook at https://www.facebook.com/OBooks
and Twitter at https://twitter.com/obooks.